Manufactured in the United States of America

GEOFFREY CHAUCER

by Nevill Coghill

SIR THOMAS MALORY

by M. C. Bradbrook

British writers and Their work.

UNIVERSITY OF NEBRASKA PRESS · LINCOLN

PREFACE

BRITISH WRITERS AND THEIR WORK is addressed to the student who wants a general introduction to a particular writer or group of writers, and also to the more advanced student and to the lover of literature who enjoy fresh, thoughtful literary criticism. Each volume includes essays on from two to six writers, the series as a whole being planned to consider British men of letters from the fourteenth century to the present day. The essays in most instances combine the biography of a writer with a critical appreciation of his work. Many of the contributors are themselves well-known English authors and critics.

The essays originally were published separately for The British Council under the titles listed on the copyright page. They are reprinted in the American edition with minor corrections.

It is hoped that not only will the essays prove useful and stimulating, but that the select bibliographies will make each volume a convenient, portable reference work. While the arrangement will vary somewhat from volume to volume, each essay usually is followed by a full list of the first editions of the writer's works (provided as a complement to the account in the essay); a list of collected editions, modern reprints, and student editions; a list of bibliographies and reference works; and a list of critical and biographical studies (including both standard works and other works found especially useful by the author of the essay). Each volume ordinarily concludes with a list of general works. The select bibliographies, compiled by the editor of the American edition, are based on the bibliographies originally published with the essays.

J. W. R.

CONTENTS

GEOFFREY CHAUCER

by Nevill Coghill

CHAUCER

Engraved by J. Thomson (1788–1850) from the marginal portrait in a 15th-century manuscript (British Museum: Harley MS.4866, f.88) of Occleve's *De Regimine Principum*.

GEOFFREY CHAUCER was born in London towards the year 1340 or a little later, certainly not later than 1345. He died on 25 October 1400, and was buried in Westminster Abbey. Other main dates in his life are:

1357   Page or henxman in the household of the Countess of Ulster.

1359   Taken prisoner at 'Retters' on a military expedition to France.

1360   Ransomed and returned to England.
           Carried letters for the King to France.

Between 1360 and 1366 may have spent some time in study at the Inner Temple.

1366   or earlier, married Philippa de Roet.

1367   In the service of King Edward III, described as *dilectus valettus noster* ('our dearly beloved valet').

1369   On military service in France, perhaps with John of Gaunt. Death of Blanche, Duchess of Lancaster, John of Gaunt's first wife. Composed *The Book of the Duchess*.

1370   Abroad in the King's service.

1371–2   In London.

1372   First mission to Italy (to Genoa and Florence; possibly to Padua). Returns in following year to London.

1374   Comptroller of the Customs and Subsidy of Wools, Skins and Tanned Hides in London.

1375   Received wardship of Edward Staplegate.

1376   Received grant of the amount ($£71$ 4s. 6d.) paid in fine by John Kent for evading duty on wool.

1377   On missions to Flanders and to France.
           (*Death of Edward III, accession of Richard II.*)

1378   Second mission to Italy (Milan).
           Returns to London.

1382   Comptroller of the Petty Customs of London.

1385   Permitted to employ a Deputy.
           Justice of the Peace for Kent.

1386   Knight of the Shire for Kent, sits in Parliament of Westminster.
           Gives evidence in the Scrope-Grosvenor case (October).
           (*John of Gaunt abroad.*) Loses both his Comptrollerships (December).

1387   (?) Death of Philippa Chaucer.

1388   Pressed for money.

1389   (*John of Gaunt returns to England.*) Chaucer made Clerk of the King's Works.

1390   Put on a commission to repair the banks of the Thames between Woolwich and Greenwich.

1391   Appointed Sub-Forester of North Petherton Park (a sinecure?).
           Loses his Clerkship.

1394   In straitened circumstances, receives pension from the King, and is under pressure from creditors for some time.

1398   Granted an annual hogshead of wine by the King for life.

1399   (*Richard II deposed and murdered. Accession of Henry IV.*)
           Previous pension confirmed to Chaucer and an additional grant made to him by the new King.
           Chaucer leases a house in the garden of St. Mary's, Westminster, on Christmas Eve.

1400   Last recorded date on which his pension was paid, 5 June.
           25 October death and burial in Westminster Abbey.

GEOFFREY CHAUCER

I

LONDON-BORN

A shilling life will give you all the facts.
W. H. Auden

IN what his father and mother would have regarded as his career—for it was they who had the wit, and the luck, to launch him upon it—Geoffrey Chaucer did remarkably well. His successive appointments, missions and awards, achieved in the administrative service of three kings, was something better than a mediocre success; and who could have foreseen that his marriage, prudent and suitable as it was, romantic too, for all we know to the contrary, would ultimately make him brother-in-law to his own best patron, John of Gaunt, that is to the fourth son of Edward III, the uncle of Richard II and the father of Henry IV, the poet's chief employers?

But it was not as a poet that they employed him; his poetry was an extra, so far as they were concerned. His career was that of a courtier, as his father and mother had intended, and it was that career that gained him his place in the official records of the time; except for them, we should probably know as little about him as we do of the other great poets of his age, the authors of *Piers Plowman* and of *Sir Gawain*.

Yet the recorded facts of this courtier's life, remote from poetry as they may seem, are those upon which the styles of his poetry turn; they mark its progress from his first beginnings, step by step, to his maturities. Being a courtier made a European of him, and more than that; he became the first great English poet in the general tradition of Christendom, the heir of Ovid, of Vergil, of Boethius; of St. Jerome, of de Lorris and de Meun, of Dante and Boccaccio.

He was not our first great Christian poet; Langland was

7

before him. But he was our first poet in the high culture of Europe, then breaking out all over England in glorious profusion of creative power. There are moments in the lives of nations when they declare their genius: the life of Geoffrey Chaucer fell in the middle of our first such moment.

In every art then known, and in some now lost, in architecture, sculpture, carving and stained glass; in the work of goldsmiths and armourers and of the makers of robes for ceremonial and daily use, in manuscript illumination, painting and portraiture, music and dancing, sudden perfections were being achieved all over the country. Moreover, they were harmonious with each other, as if there were a general sense of a particular style, and a very free flowering of it in every field. Grace, strength, freshness of invention, clarity, richness, and a sense of the humane as well as of the divine characterize this breeding-time of our first civilization.

Out of the multitude of masterpieces I will name a few to show these qualities: the central tower of Wells Cathedral and the breath-taking inverted arch that supports it; the work of William Joy about the year of Chaucer's birth (c. 1340): the great octagonally-fashioned vault over the transept of Ely Cathedral, the work of Alan of Walsingham and William Hurley not long before, miracles, both, of strength and ingenuity: the nave of Westminster Abbey, grove of slender stone, built by the greatest English architect before Wren, Henry Yevele. Chaucer, late in his life, knew and worked with him. It was Yevele who, with Hugh Herland, Master-Carpenter, also gave us Westminster Hall (1394).

In portraiture, an art then dawning and of which Chaucer too became a master, we may think of the tragic alabaster face of Edward II that haunts the visitor to Gloucester Cathedral, or the knowingly practical visage of Henry IV, carved in Canterbury; less tragic than Edward, more humane than Henry, the painted effigy of Edward, Lord Despenser, kneeling in his chantry-roof in Tewkesbury Abbey. Illumination and painting could show pieces as fine as these:

instance the Wilton Diptych that presents the young Richard II to the Blessed Virgin and a host of angels, himself hardly less angelical in beauty; or the greater portrait of him that hangs in Westminster Abbey and shows him against a gold background in a robe the colour of dry blood. From his face, he seems to be thinking Shakespearian thoughts.

In glass the ante-chapel windows of New College by Thomas of Oxford, with their canopied saints and patriarchs in soft greens and porphyries and blues, seem a silent reproach to the baroque-souled figures and inharmonious tints of a neighbouring window by Sir Joshua Reynolds, that was somehow allowed to be put there in an age that knew no better. In the same chapel is the crozier of William of Wykeham, a master-work of the goldsmiths, silversmiths and enamellers of the fourteenth century.

Harp and flute and social song were part of a gentleman's education (as we shall see) and song was gracefully combined with dance in the 'carol'; the art of conversation was so much esteemed that Andreas Capellanus gives it third place among the requirements for a girl worthy to be loved, and Chaucer, in his first considerable poem, ensures that it shall be known to have graced the dead patroness he is celebrating, Blanche, Duchess of Lancaster:

> And which a goodly, softe speche
> Had that swete, *my lyves leche*![1]
> So frendly, and so well ygrounded,
> *Up*[2] *al resoun* so wel yfounded
> And *so tretable*[3] to alle goode[4]

In poetry (our chief concern in this essay) the age was richer than in all else, except architecture. There were the three great poets I have mentioned, of whom Chaucer was chief; there was John Gower too, and the makers of our Miracle Cycles, then coming to their first fullness in York and elsewhere. *Troilus & Criseyde, The Canterbuty Tales, Piers*

[1] My life's physician.   [2] Upon all reason.   [3] So tractable.
[4] All Chaucer quotations are from F. N. Robinson's edition, 1933.

Plowman, Sir Gawain, Pearl, and *The Wakefield Miracle Cycle* may speak for the great achievements of those times in poetry, but there was also a first pouring forth of lyrical writing, by many anonymous hands and one-poem men, of whose work here is a fragment:

> Bytuene Mersh and Aueril,
>   When spray biginneth to springe,
> The lutel foul hath hire wyl
>   On hyre lud to synge,
>   Ich libbe in loue-longinge
>   For semlokest of alle thynge:
>   (S)he may me blisse bringe;
> Icham in hire bandoun.
>   *An hendy hap ichabbe yhent;*
>   *Ichot from heuene it is me sent;*
>   *From alle wymmen mi loue is lent,*
>   *And lyht on Alysoun.*

> (Sisam, *Fourteenth Century Verse and Prose*)

(Between March and April, when the spray begins to spring, the little bird has its pleasure to sing in its language. I live in love-longing for the seemliest of all things; may (s)he bring me joy; I am in her power. I have grabbed a lucky chance, I know it has been sent me from Heaven; from all women my love has turned away, and lights on Alison.)

and here another, in a more 'metaphysical' vein:

> Gold & al this werdis wyn
> Is nouth but cristis rode;
> I wolde ben clad in cristis skyn,
> That ran so longe on blode,
> & gon t'is herte & taken myn In—
> Ther is a fulsum fode.

(Carleton Brown, *Religious Lyrics of the Fourteenth Century*)

(Gold and all the glory of this world is nought, save Christ's cross; I would be clad in Christ's skin, that ran so long with blood, and go to his heart and make my Inn there, where there is a bounteous food.)

This was a mystical age, the age of Richard Rolle and Juliana of Norwich; her writings are like the writings of a lover:

> I saw his sweet face as it were dry and bloodless with pale dying. And later, more pale, dead, languoring; and then turned more dead unto blue: and then more brown-blue, as the flesh turned more deeply dead. For his Passion shewed to me most specially in his blessed face, and chiefly in his lips: there I saw these four colours, though it were afore fresh, ruddy, and liking, to my sight.

It was also an age that loved learning, a founding-time of Colleges. Nine new ones were added within the century, four at Oxford and five at Cambridge.

Paradoxes are to be understood as best they can. This same age of our first, and in some ways our finest, culture, was also an age pre-eminent for plague, poverty, rebellion, war (both international and civil), political murder, heresy and schism. Fissures seemed to be opening in the Catholic Church with the 'Babylonish' captivity of the Popes at Avignon, followed by a great schism and war between Pope and Anti-Pope. To Langland it seemed like the Day of Anti-Christ. Heresies were also raising their terrible heads; the chronicles tell the story of a knight who snatched the consecrated host out of his priest's hand and fled away with it, to devour it with oysters and mustard, thinking (in some obscure way) that this disproved Transubstantiation.

There were secular terrors too: the Black Death began its repeated visitations in 1348, when Chaucer was a child.

> Ther cam a privee theef, men clepeth Deeth,[1]
> That in this contree all the peple sleeth.
>
> (*The Pardoner's Tale*)

The tyrannies of nature were matched by the tyrannies of man. Mob-madness and xenophobia filled London with the shouts and shrieks of massacre when the rebels of The Peasants' Revolt, entering London, fell upon the Flemings

[1] There came a secret thief that men call death.

there in 1381; Chaucer, in later years, passed it off as a joke, a farmyard flurry:

> Certes, he Jakke Straw and his meynee[1]
> Ne made nevere shoutes half so shrille,
> Whan that they wolden any Flemyng kille,
> As thilke day was maad upon the fox . . .
>
> (Nun's Priest's Tale)

This Revolt, which was also an attack upon Church and Law, was suppressed as savagely as it had arisen, with hanging in chains for many a deluded peasant. Their betters were also liable to liquidation; the intrigues that stewed with and seethed outside the Court and government led often enough to the scaffold:

> The ax was sharpe, the stokke was harde
> In the xiiii yere of Kyng Richarde.
>
> (Sisam, Fourteenth Century Verse and Prose)

As a sort of ground-bass to all these disturbances, there was an unstaunched issue of blood, bitter, barbarous and futile, in the feuds with France that are now called The Hundred Years' War. No doubt it was conducted with great *panache* and had moments of thrilling, heraldic heroism; it certainly dazzled the eyes of its chronicler, Froissart, who could write of it with the kind of romantic feeling that stirs in us when we read Chaucer's *Knight's Tale:*

> Thus the knights and squires sparkled abroad in the plain and fought together . . . —(Froissart, 1364)
>
> It was great joy to see and consider the banners and the penons and the noble armoury . . . the Prince himself[2] was the chief flower of chivalry of all the world, and had with him as then right noble and valiant knights and squires . . . —(1367)
>
> The men of arms beat down the Flemings on every side . . . and as the Flemings were beaten down, there were pages ready to cut their throats with great knives, and so slew them without pity, as though they had been but dogs . . . —(1382)

---

[1] And his gang.   [2] The Black Prince.

What with Jakke Straw and the men of arms, the Flemings met with small mercy, but nationalism knows no restraint and soldiers cannot expect a ransom from a Flemish burgher.

Into this age of extremes, which in every direction forces superlatives from its astonished student, Geoffrey Chaucer, most equable of men, was born.

He was born in the middle of the century and in the middle of society, towards the year 1340, in a middle-class cockney home. No record was kept of the event. Round the corner, and half a street away from his father's house, flowed the Thames; a little above towered old St. Paul's, whose chapter-house and cloister, the work of William Ramsey, stood in their brand-new perpendicular beauty. A new style had been born.

II

EDUCATION IN RHETORIC

The noble rethor poete of brytayne
(John Lydgate: *Life of Our Lady*,
referring to Chaucer)

Not far away, in the Vintry, stood St. Paul's Almonry; and if it is not a fact, it is a likely conjecture that young Geoffrey was sent there daily to learn his letters and his Latin, through the medium of French:

Children in scole, ayenst the vsage and manere of alle othere naciouns beeth compelled for to leue hire owne langage, and for to construe hir lessouns and here thynges in Frensche, and so they haueth seth the Normans come first to Engelong. Also gentil men children beeth i-taught to speke Frensche from the tyme that they beeth i-rokked in here cradel . . . And vplondisshe men wil likne hym self to gentil men, and fondeth with greet besynesse for to speke Frensce, *for to be i-tolde of.*

(Higden, *Polychronicon*, 1363)

As might be expected from the above, Chaucer's *Squire* in *The Canterbury Tales*, being of 'gentil' birth, was accustomed to speaking French, and confesses:

> Myn Englissh eek is insufficient

and the *Franklin*, an 'vplondisshe' or country-bred man if ever there was one, loudly regrets that his own son lacks the gentle breeding of the *Squire*, in such a way as to unleash the mockery of the Host, who could see at a glance that there was a penny short in the shilling of the *Franklin's* gentility:

> 'Straw for youre gentillesse!' quod oure Hoost.

What was it like to be at school in those days? Children were sent very young: *enfantz*, they were called, and their instruction began like that of Chaucer's 'litel clergeon' in *The Prioress's Tale*, with the singing of Latin hymns, the easiest way into the difficult language of Heaven:

> I lerne song, I kan but smal grammeere.
>
> *(Prioress's Tale)*

At Westminster School, and probably at St. Paul's too, a boy who knew Latin and presumed to speak English or even French, had a cut of the cane for every word so spoken. Rod and birch were frequently applied to the seat of learning and accepted as a rueful joke by the little victims. There is, for instance, a late fifteenth-century poem by—or, at least, about—a boy who had tried to excuse himself for being late for school on the grounds that his mother had told him to go out and milk the ducks:

> My master lokith as he were madde:
> 'wher hast *thou* be, thow sory ladde?'
> 'Milked dukkis, my moder badde:'
> hit was no mervayle thow I were sadde.
>> what vaylith it me thowgh I say nay?
> My master pepered my ars with well good spede . . .
> he wold not leve till it did blede,
> Myche sorow haue he for his dede!
>
> *(Babees Book*, ed. F. J. Furnivall)

Discipline, if rough, was ready. The day began with prayer, then a recitation of the Creed, the Lord's Prayer, a Salutation to the Blessed Virgin and some psalm-singing, which was called 'dinging on David'. And so to class to learn your letters, to do sums with counters, to Grammar, to Logic, to Rhetoric and to the Classic authors, Ovid, Vergil, Lucan, Cicero, Statius, Dionysius Cato and the rest.

Rhetoric has come to mean a windy way of speech, marked by a pompous emptiness and insincerity, and trotted out as a trick on any occasion calling for solemn humbug. It did not mean this to the Middle Ages. To them it meant the whole craft of writing, the arts and devices by which whatever you had to say could best be varied, clarified and elaborated; it even included the study of appropriate gesture.

> And, for his tale sholde seme the bettre,
> Accordant to his wordes was his cheere,
> As techeth art of speche hem that it leere.
>
> *(The Squire's Tale)*

> (He suited his action to his words, as the art of speech teaches those that learn it, to do.)

The word *rhetor* had come to be used as the simple equivalent of 'good poet'; so Chaucer used it in *The Squire's Tale*, to underline the skill needed to describe the beauty of his heroine:

> It moste been a rethor excellent . . .
> If he sholde hire descryven every part.
> I am noon swich, I moot speke as I kan.

So it was used of Chaucer by Lydgate and other poets:

> O reverend Chaucere, rose of rethoris all,
> As in oure tong ane flour imperiall . . .
>
> (William Dunbar, *The Golden Targe*)

The rules of rhetoric are now, for the most part, forgotten, and the enormous effect they had on the formation of Chaucer's style is therefore often not perceived, even by good Chaucerists. Every educated person in the fourteenth century knew them and admired those who knew how to use them, of whom Chaucer was chief. It would be fair to say that an anthology of the finest things in Chaucer could be used as a means of demonstrating the nature and use of these rules.

They had come down from Roman times and reached a second flowering in the twelfth and thirteenth centuries. The scholars of that time, notably Matthieu de Vendôme (c. 1170) and Geoffrey de Vinsauf (c. 1210) had assembled all the traditions of rhetoric in a number of prose treatises and illustrative verses; the general heading under which particular devices of style were recommended, was that of *Amplificatio*, the art of enlarging and embellishing your matter. There were eight or ten principal ways of doing so, each with its high-sounding name, and some with as many as four subdivisions. To take a few examples, there was *Circumlocutio*, the art of making a simple statement in a roundabout and decorative way:

> The bisy larke, messager of day,
> Salueth in hir song the morwe gray,
> And firy Phebus riseth up so bright
> That al the orient laugheth of the light,
> And with his stremes dryeth in the greves[1]
> The silver dropes hangynge on the leves.
>
> (*The Knight's Tale*)

The simple statement underlying this lovely and lively passage is 'The sun rose brightly'. That Chaucer was perfectly conscious of this and, sometimes also amused by it, can be seen from:

> But sodeynly bigonne revel newe
> Til that the brighte sonne loste his hewe,
> For th'orisonte hath reft the sonne his lyght—
> This is as muche to saye as it was nyght.

The first twelve, magical lines of the *Prologue* to *The*

---

[1] Groves.

Canterbury Tales is a simple *circumlocutio* for 'In mid-april, people go on pilgrimage'.

Another figure of rhetoric, much used by Chaucer, was *Interpretatio;* this consisted in repeating an idea in other words: *varius sis et tamen idem.*[1]

A plain example of this would be:

> Soun ys noght but eyr ybroken,
> And every speche that ys spoken,
> Lowd or pryvee, foul or fair,
> In his substaunce ys but air . . .
>
> (*House of Fame*, II)

The last three lines are an *Interpretatio* of the first. But the figure could also have a subtler form, as when the idea was not only repeated, but given a new twist, for instance:

> Ful swetely herde he confessioun,
> And pleasaunt was his absolucioun:
> He was an esy man to yeve penaunce,
> Ther as he wiste to have a good pitaunce.
>
> (*The Prologue*)

The last two lines repeat the sense of the first with a dagger-thrust of meaning added.

In like manner examples of every figure of rhetoric can currently be found in Chaucer: of *Digressio* in its two forms, namely when you digress to matter outside your story in order to illuminate it (as when the *Wife of Bath* tells the story of Midas to illustrate a point in her own tale) or when you digress by developing an idea within your story, in a manner directly arising from it (as when the *Merchant* in describing the garden that Old January had made, digresses to thoughts of the *Romance of the Rose*, Priapus and Proserpina). Or of *Occupatio*, when you explain that you are too busy to go into details; this can be used, either to shorten your tale:

> I coude folwe, word for word, Virgile.
> But it wolde lasten al to longe while.
>
> (*Legend of Good Women*)

[1] Be various and yet the same (de Vinsauf: *De Poetria Nova*).

or to lengthen it, by saying you have no time to describe the things which you then proceed to describe:

> . . . And eek it nedeth nat for to devyse
> At every cours the ordre of hire servyse.
> I wol nat tellen of hir strange sewes,[1]
> Ne of hir swannes, ne of hire heronsewes,[2]
> Eek in that lond, as tellen knyghtes olde,
> Ther is som mete that is ful deynte holde,
> That in this lond men recche of it but smal;[3]
> Ther nys no men that may reporten al.

> (*The Squire's Tale*)

The *Squire's* use of *Occupatio* is tame, however, compared to that of his father the *Knight*, who performs a dazzling cadenza of some fifty lines towards the end of his tale, enumerating all the features of Arcite's funeral which (he says) he has no time to mention. It is a real *tour de force*.

But Chaucer's favourite rhetorical device was certainly *Apostrophatio*. This figure had four subdivisions, of which the commonest was *Exclamatio*, a simple exclamation of feeling, of whatever kind; the second and third, *Subjectio*, and *Dubitatio*, were forms of rhetorical question, and the last, *Conduplicatio*, a series of exclamations each beginning with the same phrase; this Chaucer only uses in his most serious invocations:

> Lo here, of payens corsed olde rites,[4]
> Lo here, what alle hire goddes may availle!
> Lo here, these wrecched worldes appetites!
> Lo here, the fyn and guerdoun for travaille[5]
> Of Jove, Apollo, of Mars, of swich rascaille!

> (*Troilus & Criseyde*, V)

Chaucer sparkles with apostrophes; he is ever ready to exclaim in sympathy, wonder, indignation, pathos, prayer and

---

[1] Strange broths.   [2] Their young heron (like the swans, a dish to eat).
[3] In this country people think little of it.
[4] Behold the accursed, ancient rites of pagans.
[5] Behold the end and the reward for your labours (given by Jove, etc.).

irony, to address his audiences personally with a question not meant to be answered, but which brings them into the story:

> Woot ye nat where there stant a litel toun
> Which that ycleped is Bobbe-up-and-doun,
> Under the Blee, in Canterbury weye?
> (*The Manciple's Prologue*)

or to picture an incident in a tale by reminding them of something similar in their own lives, as when he asks them to imagine the plight of his heroine by recalling the sight of some unhappy criminal on his way to execution:

> Have ye nat seyn somtyme a pale face,
> Among a prees,[1] of hym that hath be lad
> Towards his deeth, wher as hym gat no grace,
> And switch a colour in his face hath had,
> Men myghte knowe his face that was bistad,[2]
> Amonges all the faces in that route?
> So stant Custance, and looketh hire aboute.
> (*The Man of Law's Tale*)

These are rhetorical questions, not exactly of the kinds named above, but of a kind to vary, by an apostrophe to his hearers, his means of engaging their attention. Often he will pause in mid-story to ask what sort of a universe it can be where such things happen, or to make a general comment on life:

> Allas, allas, that ever love was sinne!
> (*Wife of Bath's Prologue*)

These were things which Chaucer began to learn in his schooldays, and in his hands the rules of the pedants became the instruments of a living and natural style; as with any great virtuoso, the technical rule or accomplishment, artificial and laborious as it may seem, can become the means of

---

[1] Crowd.   [2] Set round (with enemies).

a greater freedom of expression, can even prompt a thought
that might have been lost without it, for

> . . . Nature is made better by no mean
> But Nature makes that mean: so, over that art
> Which you say adds to Nature, is an art
> That Nature makes.
>
> *(The Winter's Tale)*

Above all, Chaucer's training in rhetoric sharpened his
perception of character; no one was his equal in this, because
no one had his touch with the rhetorical figure of *Descriptio*.
This is a figure to which we must return later. At the
moment let us pass on from St. Paul's Almonry (if that
indeed was where he had his early schooling) and follow him
into the next phase of his up-bringing. It was the decisive
phase, the true beginning of his career as a courtier, and as
a poet.

III

EDUCATION IN COURTESY

> Let me see if Philip can
> Be a little gentleman.
>
> Heinrich Hoffman: *Struwwelpeter*

At some unknown date but certainly when he was still a
boy, Geoffrey was taken from school and put out to service
in the household of Elisabeth, Countess of Ulster. She was
the wife of Lionel, third son of Edward III and later Duke of
Clarence. For Geoffrey this was an almost unimaginable
stroke of good fortune; his parents, no doubt through their
slender court connections, had somehow pulled it off.

The Countess kept household books, on parchment.
These books were later torn up and the parchment was used
to line a manuscript of poems by Lydgate and Hoccleve. A

nineteenth-century scholar, examining the manuscript, discovered the lining. It was found to contain the first known reference to Geoffrey Chaucer. It is dated April 1357 and records that the Countess laid out seven shillings on a cloak and a pair of red-and-black breeches for the lad. He had taken the first step in courtiership and was a page in a royal household.

This did not mean that his education was interrupted; on the contrary, it was widened, intensified and given a practical turn. We know almost exactly what it consisted of, thanks to another household book, the *Liber Niger* of Edward IV, in which is laid down the traditional curriculum for lads in his position, rising from page to squire. They were known as henxmen or henchmen, a word derived from the older word *hengest* meaning a horse; for all chivalry (to which Chaucer was now apprenticed) arises from the cult of the horse as the word *cheval* implies; it tamed and civilized the lust of battle much in the way that courtly love tamed and civilized the lust of the body; the tournament was the meeting-place of both, and it did what it could to impart to the natural Yahoo some qualities of the Houyhnhnm.

Edward IV arranged for 'young gentylmen, Henxmen, VI Enfauntes or more, as it shall please the Kinge' to be placed under the tuition of a Maistyr of Henxmen

> to shew the schooles[1] of urbanitie and nourture of Englond, to lerne them to ryde clenely and surely; to drawe them also to justes (*jousting*); to lerne them were theyre harneys (*to teach them how to wear their equipment, armour etc*); to have all curtesy in wordes, dedes and degrees (*i.e. to know who ranks above or below whom, as Griselda did in the Clerk's Tale, welcoming her lord's guests 'everich in his degree'*) . . . Moreover to teche them sondry languages, and othyr lerninges vertuous, to harping, to pype, sing, daunce, and with other honest and temperate behaviour and patience . . . and eche of them to be used to that thinge of vertue that he shall be moste apt to lerne (*i.e. to be encouraged in any personal talent*), with remembraunce dayly of Goddes servyce accustumed. This maistyr sittith in the halle,

[1] Scholars?

next unto these Henxmen . . . to have his respecte unto theyre demeanynges (*attend to their behaviour*), and to theyre communication (*conversation*) . . .

The best results of such a system can be seen in Chaucer's *Knight* and *Squire*; and, as I think, in Chaucer too.

Courtesy, it will be noticed, is the first thing to be stressed in this schedule of breeding, after the military essential of horsemanship. Courtesy is behaviour proper to a Court, and the masters in courtesy fixed their standards by the highest Court they knew of, which was the Court of Heaven. That was the Court, they claimed, in which courtesy had its origin:

> Clerkys that canne the scyens seuene,
> Seys that cuttasy came fro heuen
> When gabryell owre lady grette,
> And elyzabeth with here mette.
> All vertus be closyde in curtasy,
> An Alle vyces in vilony.

(The Young Children's Book)

(Learned men that know the seven sciences say that courtesy came from Heaven when Gabriel greeted Our Lady and Elizabeth met with her. All virtues are included in courtesy, and all vices in rusticity, *Vilony* is a difficult word to translate. It is here intended to mean a condition of primitive rustic malice, ignorance and crudity, to be presumed of a countryman in a savage semi-animal state. *Villanus* means someone living in the wilds as opposed to *civis*, a city-dweller versed in 'urbanitie' (*urbs* = a city).

Of all our poets, Geoffrey Chaucer is the most courteous to those who read or listen to him; he seems ever-conscious of our presence and charmed to be in such perceptive company. He never threatens or alarms us, as Milton can, intent upon his great theme; nor ignores us, as Wordsworth can, intent upon himself. He addresses his readers as if he could wish for none better, he exchanges experiences with them, consults them, and begs them not to take offence at what he is about to say, touching his show of courtesy with an elegant but ironic wit:

> But first I pray yow, of youre curteisye,
> That ye n'arette[1] it nat my vileynye,
> Thogh that I pleynly speke in this mateere,
> To telle yow hir wordes and hir cheere . . .
> Whoso shal telle a tale after a man,
> He moot reherce as ny as evere he kan
> Everich a word, if it be in his charge,
> Al speke he never so rudeliche and large,
> Or ellis he moot telle his tale untrewe,
> Or feyne thyng, or fynde wordes newe.
> He may nat spare, althogh he were his brother;
> He moot as wel seye o word as another.
> Crist spak hymself ful brode[2] in hooly writ,
> And wel ye woot no vileynye is it.
>
> *(Prologue to the Canterbury Tales)*

Chaucer learnt his manners not only from those with whom he came in contact, but also from cautionary rhymes, of which there survive a great number, specially written for the education of children. They are too long to quote in full, for they enter into details of table-manners, right down to versified instructions for the washing of spoons and the laying of cloths, freely intermingled with moral advice:

> . . . Loke thyne hondis be wasshe clene,
> That no fylthe on thy nayles be sene.
> Take thou no mete tylle grace be seyde,
> And tylle thou see alle thyng arayede . . .
> And at thy mete, yn the begynnyng,
> Loke on pore men that thow thynk,
> For the fulle wombe without any faylys[3]
> Wot fulle lytyl what the hungery aylys.
> Ete not thy mete so hastely,
> Abyde and ete esily . . .
>
> *(The Lytylle Childrenes Lytil Boke or Edyllys be[4])*

---

[1] Impute it not.   [2] Very broadly.
[3] For the full stomach, without fail, knows very little of what the hungry one is suffering.   [4] 'Ere they become noble'?

Perhaps the best of these poems is the one called *The Babees Book;* it is addressed to children of the blood royal, and like other poems in this vein, gives precise instructions how to behave:

> Youre heede, youre hande, your feet, hold yee in reste
> Nor thurhe clowyng your flesshe loke yee nat Rent;[1]
> Lene to no poste whils that ye stande present
> Byfore your lorde . . .

and so forth; and thus it ends:

> And, swete children, for whos love now I write,
> I yow beseche withe verrey lovande herte,
> To knowe this book that yee sette your delyte;
> And myhtefulle god, that suffred peynes smerte,
> In curtesye he make yow so experte,
> That thurhe your nurture and youre governaunce
> In lastynge blysse yee mowe your self avaunce!

In opening a window upon the Middle Ages, there is always the danger that it may turn into a stained glass window, nevertheless I am forced by all these cautionary verses to believe that the reason for being courteous was a religious reason, namely that it was pleasing to God and would advance your soul; it was the application of Christianity to social behaviour, a practical way of learning to love your neighbour as yourself. *Manners makyth Man.*

The simple piety of this approach to courtesy was no doubt dinned into the little bourgeois boy from the moment he entered the Ulster household. Although there were rules of thumb for courtesy, the underlying theory had been worked out by the philosophers and poets. Indeed, when he grew up, Chaucer himself, as we shall see, made a significant contribution to it.

The problem was one with which the age was profoundly concerned. What is nobility? How does one become noble? Has it to do with wealth or heredity?

> Whan Adam dalf and Eve span
> Who was tho the gentilman?

[1] See that you do not tear yourself by scratching.

This watchword of The Peasants' Revolt had come to them (though they knew it not) from Dante, who had devoted an entire treatise to the subject:

> If Adam himself was noble, we are all noble, and if he was base, we are all base.
>
> *(Convivio,* Treatise IV, Ch. **xv**)

Dante was arguing that nobility was not inherited. In this he was echoing Boethius some eight hundred years before

> yif thou ne have no gentilesse of thiself . . . foreyn gentilesse ne maketh thee nat gentil.
>
> (Boethius: *De Consolatione Philosophie* **III** prose vi, translated by Chaucer)

Nor, said Dante, had nobility anything to do with wealth. It was wholly a matter of virtue, he argued, following Aristotle in his argument:

> . . . this word 'nobleness' means the perfection in each thing of its own proper nature . . . everything is most perfect when it touches and reaches it own proper virtue . . . So the straight path leads us to look for this definition . . . by way of the fruits; which are moral and intellectual virtues whereof this our nobleness is the seed . . .
>
> *(Convivio,* IV, xvi)

Chaucer had read and alludes to this discussion in the *Convivio,* but in giving his own account of 'gentilesse' (or as we would say, 'nobility') he appeals to higher authority than Dante, or Aristotle either. To be 'gentil', he says, is to imitate Christ, for that is the perfection of our proper natures.

> But, for ye speken of swich gentillesse
> As is descended out of old richesse,
> That therfore sholden ye be gentil men,
> Swich arrogance is nat worth an hen.
> Looke who that is moost vertuous alwey,
> Pryvee and apert,[1] and moost entendeth ay

[1] In private and public.

To do the gentil dedes that he kan;
Taak hym for the grettest gentil man.
Crist wole we clayme of hym our gentillesse,
Nat of oure eldres for hire old richesse . . .

(Wife of Bath's Tale)

This, the root of all things, was for Chaucer the root from which the flowers of charity and courtesy both sprang, and like sainthood, they might be met with in every rank of society. The rough-mouthed Host himself was capable of it:

. . . And with that word he sayde,
As curteisly as it had been a mayde,
'My lady Prioresse, by youre leve,
So that I wiste I sholde yow nat greve,
I wolde demen that ye tellen sholde
A tale next, if so were that ye wolde.
Now wol ye vouche sauf, my lady deere?'

But the finest figure of courtesy in *The Canterbury Tales* is the *Knight*. Chaucer was very careful to make this noble figure as realistic as any of his rogues; half the details of his career, as it is epitomized in the *Prologue*, were fresh in Chaucer's mind from the Scrope-Grosvenor trial of 1386, in the course of which the Scrope family, bearing the disputed arms (*azure a bend or*), had been seen in 'the great sea', at Satalye, at Alexandria, in Spain, Prussia and Lithuania (Lettowe). All these place-names occur in the *Prologue*, written in the same year, in the description of the *Knight's* military career; nothing said of him could have sounded more likely or authentic to Chaucer's first hearers; his 'character' would have sounded equally so, formed as it was on the principles of Christian courtesy dinned into everyone day in and day out from childhood. The entire knightly caste had been brought up that way for some two centuries and was to be brought up so for at least a century more.

Chaucer's *Knight* is the embodiment of a whole way of life, a creation whose importance I cannot measure or state; for it is the first image of the idea of a gentleman, in the language that has given that idea to the world. The *Knight* is to the *Plowman* as a fourteenth-century cathedral is to a fourteenth-century parish church, and all four of them were the products of the same great style and civilization.

Many things are mocked in Chaucer, but never courtesy; it was the great ideal of his age, upheld by every writer. The poet of *Sir Gawain* builds his poem upon it, to maintain in honour the Court of Arthur and the order of chivalry. If the idea was, in its origins, aristocratic, it spread outwards and downwards through society to a universal acceptance, so that the peasant Langland could think and speak of the Incarnation as the courtesy of Christ.

IV

COURTIER-SOLDIER-SCHOLAR-POET

The courtier's, soldiers', scholar's eye, tongue, sword . . .

(Hamlet)

Like many another henxman before and since, Chaucer was presently sent to the wars. It was a foul campaign, bitterly cold, utterly inept, a military fiasco; but it had one important result, it struck a blow for civilization by putting the young genius into direct touch with France and her poetry. For Chaucer's luck held; he was taken prisoner almost at once. We get a glimpse of this over his shoulder, as it were, for he tells us about it in the Scrope-Grosvenor trial already mentioned; he was one among the many witnesses. Indeed, so many and so distinguished were those called on to give evidence, a *Who's Who* for 1386 could easily be compiled from them. Chaucer deposed:

GEFFRAY CHAUCER ESQUIER del age de xl ans & plus armeez p xxvii ans pduct pr la ptie de mons Richard Lescrop jurrez & examinez demandez si lez armeez dazure ove un bende dor appteignent ou deyvent appteigner au dit mons Richard du droit & de heritage. dist q oil qar il lez ad veu estre armeez en Fraunce devant la ville de Retters . . . & . . . p tout le dit viage tanq le dit Geffrey estoit pris . . .[1]

His captivity did not last long; he was no Flemish burgher only fit to have his throat cut, but a negotiable prize. On the first of March, 1360, the King paid sixteen pounds towards his ransom. It is an old joke among the biographers of Chaucer that this was slightly less than he paid to ransom Sir Robert de Clinton's charger.

From now on Chaucer led three interweaving kinds of life, a courtier's, a scholar's and a poet's. Some chronological shape can be given to at least the first of these, the events of which help to date some of his poems, and the accessions of strength, style and subject to be discerned in them. Many are the subjects he handles; we have already touched upon one, the idea of a gentleman, and I mean to restrict myself in this essay to two more, his greatest as I think, for somewhat detailed consideration, rather than attempt in so small a space to touch on every aspect of his genius. The subjects I have chosen are those of *Love* and *Men and Women*; but before I may come to them, there is the outline of a triple life to be sketched.

For the next seven years there is no record of him as a courtier, save that he carried letters for the King to Calais at least once. But his poet's life was beginning; he was at work on a translation of the *Roman de la Rose*, transplanting an aristocratic and French philosophy of love and a French way of poetry to our native soil. He was also engaged in formal studies, too, at the Inner Temple, if we may believe a late tradition reported by Speght in his edition of Chaucer (1598)

[1] Geoffrey Chaucer Esquire, of the age of forty years and more, having borne arms for twenty-seven years, produced by Sir Richard Le Scrope's party, sworn and examined, asked if the arms of *azure with a bend or* belonged or should belong to the said Sir Richard by right and inheritance. Said that yes, for he had seen them being armed in France before the town of Retters (Rhetel, near Rheims, probably) . . . and . . . during the whole campaign when the said Geoffrey was taken prisoner . . . (*The Scrope and Grosvenor Roll*, Vol. I, edited by Sir N. H. Nicolas, 1879.)

which also asserts that he was 'fined two shillinges for beatinge a Franciscane Fryer in fletestrete'.

He was growing to manhood; all of a sudden we find him married, to a lady-in-waiting to Queen Philippa, her god-daughter perhaps, Philippa de Roet; she became Philippa Chaucer in 1366. Were they in love? We do not know; he has left us no poem to her, though he once refers to her in jest. He compares her voice awakening him in the mornings to the scream of an eagle.

In 1369, Queen Philippa died, and the Chaucers went into service with Blanche, Duchess of Lancaster, first wife of John of Gaunt. With that began (if it had not begun even earlier) the firm friendship and steady patronage that the Duke gave Chaucer ever after. Philippa Chaucer's sister, Catherine, was to become the governess of the Duke's children, then his mistress and at last his wife; so the Duke ended brother-in-law to the poet.

If the Duke did much for Chaucer, Chaucer did more for him. He made him a central and romantic figure in his first masterpiece, *The Book of the Duchess*, an elegy on the lady Blanche, who died in this very year (1369).

It is the first elegy in our language, drenched in a lesiured melancholy that begins with a dream and moves out into a great forest, to the sound of far-off hunting horns; under a tree the poet meets with a sorrowful figure in black, singing a lament for his dead lady. It is John of Gaunt, mourning the loss of Blanche, his wife. Though the poem is an elegy, it is imagined as a love-story; narrative instinct and a feeling for sexual passion (let it take what form it may) are things we learn to expect in Chaucer. This slow and dreamy poem keeps the memory of Blanche in her living grace, heroine of a tale of courtship and untimely death; the courtier and rhetor had put forth all his young art for his patron and sometime patroness.

His career as a man of affairs was now beginning; he was being used as something between a King's Messenger and a royal nuncio to France in 1370, but the great events of this kind were his missions to Italy in 1372 and 1378, for it was from these that his poetry took on much of its greatest strength.

It is worth pausing on the voyage of 1372; he went to Genoa and Florence *in nuncio regis in secretis negociis*. He was away for six months, and it is a reasonable conjecture (doubted, however, by some scholars) that he spent a part of them on a private poetical pilgrimage of his own, to visit Francis Petrarch, the most famous living poet of the day, in Padua. It would have been a rough journey, a hundred and fifty miles off-course across the Apennines in the cold and windy month of March, through a war-stricken countryside. But all that would have been nothing to a young poet (in his early thirties) eager to snatch a chance of meeting the greatest literary figure of his time.

What prompts all readers to believe he did are the lines that Chaucer was later to put into the mouth of the *Clerk of Oxford*, as he broaches the Tale of Griselda:

> I wol yow telle a tale which that I
> Lerned at Padowe of a worthy clerk,
> As preved by his werdes and his werk.
> He now is deed and nayled in his cheste,
> I prey to God so yeve his soule reste!
> Frauncers Petrak, the lauriat poete,
> Highte this clerk, whos rethorike sweete
> Enlumyned al Ytaille of poetrie . . .

Now it is a question whether what an imaginary character says in imagined circumstances is evidence of anything that happened to his imaginer in the actual world. So many authors can be shown to have used their own lives to create the lives of their characters, that it is not unreasonable to believe that Chaucer did so on this occasion, that he did indeed hear the story of Griselda from Petrarch's lips, and recorded the occasion in this oblique manner. The text of the tale, from which he came to fashion his own version, must have been subsequently acquired by him in some other way, for its date has been established as June 1374, the year of Petrarch's death. For all these possibilities, we have no proof that the two poets ever met, and it may be wisest to say, with the Sage of Cambridge:

Wovon man nicht sprechen kann, daruber muss man schweigen.[1]

In between these Italian journeys Chaucer was promoted; he became Comptroller of the Customs and Subsidies of Wools, Skins and Tanned Hides in London, and had to keep the books in his own fair hand.[2] It was a busy life and all his recreation was to read

> For when thy labour doon al ys,
> And hast mad alle thy rekenynges,
> In stede of reste and newe thynges,
> Thou goost hom to thy hous anoon,
> And, also domb as any stoon,
> Thou sittest at another book
> Tyl fully daswed is thy look.[3]

So spoke the admonishing eagle (with a voice like his wife's) in *The House of Fame*, and what the bird said need not surprise us, for Chaucer read enormously—smatteringly, perhaps, but rememberingly. Almost everything that he read seems to have left its trace upon his poetry, for he delighted in allusion and quotation (whether acknowledged or not) from his favourite authors, He drew easily on the Latin classics, Ovid, Vergil, Statius, Boethius; he was at home in the poetry of France, Deguilleville, Machault, Froissart, Deschamps and the authors of the *Roman de la Rose*. In Italian he was a reader of Dante and of Petrarch; above all he had met with at least two of Boccaccio's poems, *Il Filostrato* and the *Teseide*. Of these he made two of his own noblest works, *Troilus & Criseyde* and *The Knight's Tale*.

He was also a considerable student of the sciences,

---

[1] Ludwig Wittgenstein, *Tractatus Logico-Philosophicus:* 'What one cannot speak about, one has to keep quiet about.'

[2] And a fair hand it was, if Dr. D. J. Price is right in conjecturing that a late fourteenth-century manuscript, *The Equatorie of the Planetis*, recently brought to light by him at Peterhouse, Cambridge, is a Chaucer holograph.

[3] Till thy look is fully dazed.

especially of astronomy and mathematics; he was read in medicine, psychology and other natural sciences, including the pseudo-science of alchemy. His theology he did not so readily parade, though there is an amusing passage on God's uses for fiends in the *Friar's Tale*. He read St. Jerome and St. Bernard and could quote from almost every book in the Bible and Apocrypha. Though he may not have been the most learned, he was perhaps the most widely-read man of his day; he seems never to have lost the habit and delight of reading:

> On bokes for to rede I me delyte
> (*Prologue to the Legend of Good Women*)

There is a passage in Boswell's *Life of Johnson* describing the special powers of mind enjoyed by the Doctor; they describe Chaucer's equally well:

> . . . His superiority over other learned men consisted chiefly in what may be called the art of thinking, the art of using his mind; a certain continual power of seizing the useful substance of all that he knew and exhibiting it in a clear and forcible manner; so that knowledge, which we often see to be no better than lumber in men of dull understanding, was, in him, true, evident and actual wisdom. His moral precepts are practical; for they are drawn from an intimate acquaintance with human nature. His maxims carry conviction; for they are founded on the basis of common sense, and a very attentive and minute survey of real life . . .

It will not surprise us that Boswell adds

> His mind was so full of imagery that he might have been perpetually a poet.

To return to Chaucer's life as a courtier: he had had a windfall in the Customs in 1376; he caught out a man called John Kent evading duty on an export of wool to Dordrecht, and the culprit was fined for it to the tune of £71 4s. 6d. The whole of this sum (worth well over a thousand pounds of modern money) was paid over to Chaucer as a reward. He was becoming almost affluent. Foreign missions continued now and then to come his way, civil appointments also; in 1382 he was made Comptroller of Petty Customs, in 1385 he was allowed to appoint a deputy and was made a Justice of the Peace. In October, the following year, he sat in Parliament at Westminster as Knight of the Shire for Kent.

Then, suddenly, in 1386, fortune deserted him:

> For whan men trusteth hire, thanne wol she faille,
> And covere hire brighte face with a clowde.
>
> (*Monk's Tale*)

John of Gaunt was out of the country, and Chaucer, deprived of his patron, was deprived of his offices. He must live on his pension and on his saving until better times. In the next year Philippa died; he was now a widower with nothing to do; if this was sad for him, it was lucky for us. He began to compose *The Canterbury Tales*.

To take brief stock of his career as a writer up to the time of his wife's death, it had been fruitful of several long or fairly long poems, ambitiously different from anything ever written before in English, as well as a prose translation of Boethius's *Consolations of Philosophy* and a work of instruction in mathematics—A treatise on the Astrolabe—for 'Lyte Lowys, my sone'. There is no agreement among scholars about the dating, and little agreement about the order in which his poems were composed. We may be certain that *The Book of the Duchess* was written in 1369-70 and *The Legend of Good Women* in 1385-86; it is also sure that *Troilus &Criseyde* and such parts of his translation of the *Roman de la Rose* as have survived were written before the *Legend of Good Women*, because it mentions them; it also mentions *The Parliament of Fowls*, 'al the love of Palamon and Arcite' (later *The Knight's Tale*), the translation of Boethius, and the *Life of St. Cecilia* (later *The Second Nun's Tale*).

The Canterbury Tales (it is agreed) were begun as such towards 1386-7, and remained his 'work in progress' until the end of his life, never completed. It would seem that towards the end he tired of writing:

> For elde, that in my spirit dulleth me,
> Hath of endyting al the subtilte
> Wel nygh bereft out of my remembraunce
> (*The Complaint of Venus*)

We need not, however, take this confession too seriously; it had always been his way to make fun of himself.

Of his longer poems it only remains to mention *The House of Fame*, of which it can only be said with certainty that it was written after Chaucer had read the *Divine Comedy;* that is, at some time after his first or second visit to Italy.

His very last poem, perhaps, was a poem addressed, on the accession (1399) of the new King: it was a complaint to Chaucer's empty purse:

> I am so sory, now that ye been lyght.

It need not be taken too tragically; the poem is almost as light as the purse.

According to the inscription on his tomb, put there by a Tudor admirer, Nicholas Brigham, in 1556, Chaucer died on 25 October 1400. He was buried in Westminster Abbey; it is not known why. St. Margaret's, Westminster, was his parish church, and that would have been his natural resting-place; perhaps they put him in the Abbey because he had been Clerk of the Works, or perhaps he slipped in by some oversight, when the tumult of the new reign dwindled to a calm, much as King George III, according to Lord Byron, slipped into Heaven. It was anyhow not Chaucer's fame as a poet that made him Head of the Poets' Corner; it was not until the late sixteenth century that a corner in the Abbey began to belong to the poets.

V

THE POET OF LOVE

For I, that God of Love's servantz serve . . .

(Troilus & Criseyde, I)

From the beginning, as we have seen, Chaucer revealed himself as a love-poet and a teller of tales; to commemorate the Duchess Blanche he imagined a story about her death, told by her mourning lover in a dream-forest.

Now, in truth, this 'lover' represented John of Gaunt, Blanche's widower; they had been married ten years. In the poem, however, they are seen as courtly lovers and 'The Man in Black' voices his desire on that ideal courtly plane, in full troubadour style:

> To love hir in my beste wyse,
> To do hir worship and the servise
> That I koude thoo, be my trouthe,
> Withoute feynynge outher slouthe[1]

Troilus was later to declare his passion in the same key:

> And I to ben youre verray, humble, trewe,
> Secret, and in my paynes pacient,
> And evere mo desiren fresshly newe
> To serve, and ben ay ylike diligent . . .

(Troilus & Criseyde, III)

For a long time, true to the convention, the Man in Black dares not confess his love, and when he at last summons the courage to say the hard word, he uses the favourite in the whole vocabulary of courtly love:

> I seyde 'mercy!' and no more.

and he is refused; it is only after a conventional year of

[1] That I then could, by my truth, without pretence or sloth.

'service' that she understands and is willing to reward his sufferings:

> So whan my lady knew al this,
> My lady yaf me al hooly
> The noble yifte of hir mercy,
> Savynge hir worship, by al weyes.[1]

All that was young and romantic in Chaucer had swallowed the dream-allegories of France and the philosophy of courtly love in long draughts from the *Roman de la Rose*, the *Fontaine Amoureuse*, the *Jugement du Roi de Behaingne* and other poems of the sort, and he was trying to do extreme honour to this ordinary Christian marriage by representing it as an idealized amour; all the conventions are beautifully there, the golden hair, the gentle eyes, the neck like a tower of ivory, the long body, the white hands, the round breasts, the tints of her cheek:

> But thus moche dar I sayn, that she
> Was whit, rody, fressh, and lyvely hewed,
> And every day hir beaute newed.

It was this way of imagining love and of writing poetry that Chaucer brought back from France. Much has been written about 'courtly love' and of its sudden appearance in the courts of the nobles of Languedoc in the eleventh and twelfth centuries; some have explained it as a degenerated form of Plato's ideal affection, passed on through Arab hands to France from Africa, and, in the process, heterosexualized and allowed the gratification of the body. Be that as it may, this elegant, illicit amorism took all Christendom for its province, and our world began to ring with ballades, rondels, virelays, aubades and complaints, such as the Man in Black was singing when Chaucer came upon him in the dream-forest.

If in his youth he thought it a compliment to a bereaved

[1] My lady gave me all wholly the noble gift of her mercy, saving her honour, of course.

husband to speak of his wife as if she had been a mistress, he came ultimately to change his perspective, and his maturest expression of courtly love, *Troilus & Criseyde*, ends in the knowledge of its insufficiency.

Troilus & Criseyde was the greatest yield of his Italian journeys; he learnt from Boccaccio how to abandon dream and build a story of the waking world with clarity and realism, and yet retain within it the delicacies of feeling and convention that prevailed in the visionary, allegorical world of the *Roman de la Rose;* the new poem was undergirt by the philosophy of Boethius, who taught him the shape of tragedy and filled him with thoughts of Fortune and Free Will. For the lovers (and their mentor Pandarus) so human-free as they may seem in a thousand decisions and indecisions, move to the calls of courtly love as surely as they move under fatal stars. On the way to their still-distant doom, they pass through an ecstasy of high sexual passion, and Chaucer rises effortlessly to the great poetry of their long night of first union, which I do not know where to find equalled, except in Shakespeare, for intimacy, tenderness and noble quality; he reveals himself as *engaged* by the love he is describing:

> O blisful nyght, of hem so longe isought,
> How blithe unto hem bothe two thow weere!
> Why nad I swich oon with my soule ybought,
> Ye, or the lesste joie that was theere?[1]

Yet he retains his attitude of spectator, so typical of him:

> This Troilus in armes gan hir streyne,
>   And seyde, 'O swete, as evere mot I gon,[2]
> Now be ye kaught, now is ther but we tweyne!
> Now yeldeth yow, for other bote is non!'[3]
> To that Criseyde answerde thus anon,
> 'Ne hadde I er now, my swete herte deere,
> Ben yold, ywis, I were now nought heere!'

[1] Why had I not bought one such night at the price of my soul, yes, or the least joy that was there?

[2] As ever I may go (thrive).   [3] There is no other remedy.

O, sooth is seyd, that heled for to be
As of a fevre, or other gret siknesse,
Men moste drynke, as men may ofte se,
Ful bittre drynke; and for to han gladnesse,[1]
Men drynken ofte peyne and gret distresse;
I mene it here, as for this aventure,
That thorough a peyne hath founden al this cure.

And now swetnesse semeth more swete,
That bitternesse assaied was byforn;
For out of wo in blisse now they flete;
Non swich they felten syn that they were born.[2]
Now is this bet than bothe two be lorn.
For love of God, take every womman heede
To werken thus, if it comth to the neede.

Criseyde, al quyt from every drede and tene,[3]
As she that juste cause hadde hym to triste,
Made hym swich feste, it joye was to seene,[4]
Whan she his trouthe and clene entente wiste;
And as aboute a tree, with many a twiste,
Bytrent and writh the swote wodebynde,[5]
Gan ech of hem in armes other wynde.

And as the newe abaysed nyghtyngale,
That stynteth first whan she bygynneth to synge,
Whan that she hereth any herde tale,
And after siker doth hire vois out rynge,
Right so Criseyde, whan hire drede stente,[6]
Opned hire herte, and tolde hym hire entente . . .

. . . Hire armes smale, hir steghte bak and softe,
Hire sydes longe, flesshly, smothe and white
He gan to stroke, and good thrift bad ful ofte[7]

[1] To have gladness.   [2] None such they felt since they were born.
[3] Quite free of fear and distress.
[4] Made such a feast (welcome) for him.
[5] The sweet honey-suckle engirdles and writhes about.
[6] And as the newly abashed nightingale, that stops, as she begins to sing, when she hears any shepherd speak, and afterwards rings her voice out, just so Criseyde, when her fear ceased.
[7] And begged a blessing on her snowy throat, her breasts, round and small.

Hir snowisshe throte, hire brestes round and lite;
Thus in this hevene he gan hym to delite,
And therwithal a thousand tyme hire kiste,
That what to don, for joie unnethe he wiste . . .[1]

. . . Benigne Love, thow holy bond of thynges,
Whoso wol grace, and list the nought honouren,[2]
Lo, his desir wol fle withouten wynges . . .

(*Troilus & Criseyde, Book* III)

But from this exaltation the poem has to turn; the fatal moment must come, the lovers must part; once parted from her lover, Criseyde lacks the strength to return to him, lacks the strength to resist Diomed, is faithless. Chaucer does not reproach her; he says he would excuse her, 'for routhe', that is, for pity. At last Troilus is killed by the fierce Achilles.

Swich fyn hath, lo, this Troilus for love!
Swich fyn hath al his grete worthinesse!
Swich fyn hath his estat real above,[3]
Swich fyn his lust, swich fyn hath his noblesse!
Swich fyn hath false worldes brotelnesse!

It is the insecurity of human love in a world ruled by chance that made Chaucer see the brittleness of the courtly code. Fortune can untie the holy bond of things in human affairs, and if we seek a lasting love we must look elsewhere, to a region beyond her power:

O yonge, fresshe folkes, he or she,
In which that love up groweth with youre age,
Repeyreth hom fro worldly vanyte,
And of youre herte up casteth the visage[4]
To thilke God that after his ymage
Yow made, and thynketh al nys but a faire,
This world, that passeth soone as floures faire.

[1] He hardly knew what to do for joy.
[2] Whoso desires grace, and cares not to honour thee.
[3] His royal estate, above earth (after death).
[4] Repair home (i.e. to Heaven) from wordly vanity and cast up the countenance of your heart to that God that made you after His image.

And loveth hym, the which that right for love
Upon a crois, oure soules for to beye[1]
First starf, and roos, and sit in hevene above;
For he nyl falsen no wight, dar I seye,
That wol his herte al holly on hym leye.
And syn he best to love is, and most meeke,
What nedeth feynede loves for to seke?

What the Court held to be love, the Church held to be sin. It had a contrary love-sytem of its own. Of absolutely sovereign value in the Church's scale of sex was virginity; there was no higher kind of life than to be a virgin for the love of God. St. Jerome expressed the idea in one of his startling epigrams:

Nuptiae terram replent, virginitas paradisum.

(*Epistola adversus Jovinianum*)

(Marriages replenish the earth, virginity replenishes Paradise.)

The pre-eminence of virginity is asserted by Chaucer in *The Parson's Tale*:

Another synne of Leccherie is to bireve a mayden of hir maydenhede; for he that so dooth, certes, he casteth a mayden out of the hyeste degree that is in this present lyf... And forther over, sooth is that hooly ordre (Holy Orders) is chief of al the tresorie of God, and his especial signe and mark of chastitee ... which that is the moost precious lyf that is.

It is again asserted by the *Prioress*, in her apostrophe to the martyred chorister of her tale:

O martir, sowded to virginitee,[2]
Now maystow syngen, folwynge evere in oon[3]
The white Lamb celestial—quod she—
Of which the grete evaungelist, Seint John,
In Pathmos wroot, which seith that they that goon
Biforn this Lamb, and synge a song al newe,
That nevere, flesshly, wommen they ne knewe.[4]

[1] To buy our souls, first died and rose, and sits in Heaven above.
[2] O martyr, soldered to virginity.   [3] Continually following.
[4] That never knew women after the manner of the flesh.

It is even asserted by the *Wife of Bath*:

> Virginitee is greet perfeccion
>
> *(Wife of Bath's Prologue)*

and again,

> Crist was a mayde, and shapen as a man,
> And many a seint, sith that the world bigan;
> Yet lyvved they evere in parfit chastitee.
> I nyl envye no virginitee.

Next to virginity, the Church esteemed the condition of wedded chastity, that Shakespeare was later to celebrate allegorically in the *Threnos* of his most metaphysical poem, *The Phoenix and the Turtle;* it is a condition to which the Wife of Bath refers to, with approval, as

> continence with devocion.

and one of the first stories Chaucer ever wrote, the story of St. Cecilia (later *The Second Nun's Tale*), celebrates her sanctity in having persuaded her young and noble husband, on their wedding night and for ever after, to forgo the consummation of his love. The same idea is at the back of Chaucer's mind when, in *The Man of Law's Tale*, he feels it incumbent on him to defend his holy-hearted heroine for yielding her body to her husband; the passage rings in my ear with a note of comedy, but I am not sure if Chaucer intended it so, for it comes from his most pious period as a writer:

> They goon to bedde, as it was skile and right;[1]
> For thogh that wyves be ful hooly thynges,
> They moste take in pacience at nyght
> Swiche manere necessaries as been plesynges
> To folk that han ywedded hem with nynges,
> And leye a lite hir hoolynesse aside,
> As for the tyme—it may no bet bitide.[2]

Griselda is another chaste and patient wife; her story, enormously popular in the Middle Ages, found its fullest

---

[1] As it was reasonable and right.   [2] That is the best that can happen.

eloquence in Chaucer's telling of it. It was an earlyish work of his, and when he came back in later life to shape it for inclusion in *The Canterbury Tales,* he modified the effect of this marriage-sermon by adding an ironic tail-piece:

> It were ful harde to fynde now-a-dayes
> In al a toun Griseldis thre or two . . .

Still, virginity and chastity and married love of the kind approved by the Church, were approved in these and other of Chaucer's poems, and with no less poetry than he had celebrated courtly love. It is true that there is no sexual ecstasy recorded of the unions of Griselda or of Constance with their husbands; but then, sexual ecstasy, even in marriage, was held suspect:

> And for that many man weneth that he may nat synne for no
> likerousnesse that he dooth with his wyf, certes that opinion is fals.
>
> (*Parson's Tale*)

Over against what the Church taught and what the Troubadours taught about women, there were the opinions of the Celibate Misogynists. They reached in a long tradition from St. Jerome to Walter Map, and the extremes to which they went in vilifying the fair sex almost outdistanced the extremes of the gynecolaters in the opposite direction; as I have said before, it was an age of extremes.

The *Wife of Bath* knew all about these Children of Mercury, the natural enemies of the Children of Venus:

> The clerk, whan he is oold, and may noght do
> Of Venus werkes worth his olde sho,
> Thanne sit he doun, and writ in his dotage
> That wommen kan nat keepe hir mariage!

But, for all her low opinion of them as lovers, she admired them as debaters, and put on the whole armour of their abuse to subdue her first three husbands; her method was to anticipate the worst that could be said of women—and here she helped herself freely to St. Jerome—and fling it back scornfully at her men:

> . . . Thou seist to me it is a greet meschief
> To wedde a povre womman, for costage;
> And if that she be riche, of heigh parage,[1]
> Thanne seistow that it is a tormentrie
> To soffre hire pride and hire malencolie.
> And if that she be fair, thou verray knave,
> Thou seyst that every holour wol hire have . . .[2]
> . . . And if that she be foul, thou seist that she
> Coveiteth every man that she may se,
> For as a spanyel she wol on hym lepe,
> Til that she fynde som man hire to chepe.[3]
> Ne noon so grey goos goth ther in the lake
> As, seistow, wol been withoute make . . .[4]
> Thus seistow, lorel, whan thow goost to bedde;[5]
> And that no wys man nedeth for to wedde,
> Ne no man that entendeth unto hevene.
> With wilde thonder-dynt and firy levene
> Moote thy welked nekke be tobroke![6]

All this, and much more, that she had to say, came, almost word for word, from St. Jerome's *Epistle adversus Jovinianum* and from other 'celibate' sources.

She met her match in her fifth husband, a pretty-legged lad half her age called Jankyn (Johnnykin), with whom she was reckless enough to fall in love; this lost her the initial advantage and it was soon he, not she, that was studying the Misogynists; they became his favourite reading.

> He hadde a book that gladly, nyght and day,
> For his desport he wolde rede alway . . .
> At which book he lough alway ful faste.

---

[1] High lineage.
[2] That every lecher will have her.
[3] Some man to make a bid for her.
[4] Will be without a mate.
[5] Thus you say, you wretch.
[6] With a wild thunder-bolt and fiery lightning, may your withered neck be dashed in pieces!

It was a composite volume full of anecdote, proverb and abuse against women, and the *Wife* gives us long extracts from it; here, for instance, is an anecdote borrowed from Walter Map:

> Thanne tolde he me how oon Latumyus
> Compleyned unto his felawe Arrius
> That in his gardyn growed swich a tree
> On which he seyde how that his wyves thre
> Hanged hemself for herte despitus.[1]
> 'O leeve brother,' quod this Arrius,
> 'Yif me a plante of thilke blissed tree,
> And in my gardyn planted shal it bee!'

It was in these ways that Chaucer chose to voice the views of the Tertium Quid.

If the wondeful *Wife of Bath* seems, when we first meet with her, to have drawn her philosophy from some Cartesian well of *Copulo ergo sum*, we soon get to know her better and appreciate the complexities of her character; she can hold contradictory beliefs without the slightest inconvenience to herself, such as that virginity is a great perfection and celibacy a thing contemptible; her bullying methods with her husbands seem at first a matter of mood and idiosyncrasy, but turn out to be employed on principle, and it is this that puts her in a central position in the Great Sex War of *The Canterbury Tales*. It is fought on the issue 'Who is to have the mastery in marriage, husband or wife?'

How she handled her husbands is a lesson to every knowing woman (as she says herself) and to every man about to marry, as Chaucer said in a poem to his friend Bukton, in that momentous situation:

> The Wyf of Bathe I pray yow that ye rede . . .

In her view, it was right and proper that husbands should submit to their wives; this is not only the moral of her long

---

[1] Hanged themselves, out of the spite in their hearts.

preamble (the *Prologue* to her *Tale*) but also of the tale itself.
The point of the story is to discover what it is that women
most wish for, and the surprising answer is:

> Wommen desiren have sovereynetee
> As wel over hir housbond as hir love,
> And for to been in maistrie hym above.

Women, that is, wish for the same sovereignty over their
husbands that they exercise over their lovers; a tall order.

The challenge thus flung down by the *Wife of Bath* is
taken up first by the *Clerk of Oxford* with his tale of patient
Griselda, and her exemplary obedience to her husband;
other aspects of marriage come before us too: *The Merchant's
Tale* of January and May shows what can happen between
husband and wife when an old man marries a young girl.
The Shipman's Tale presents us with the well-known truth
that there are always half a dozen things a woman absolutely needs, to keep up with the neighbours, that she cannot
very well tell her husband about:

> And well y woot that wommen naturelly
> Desiren thynges sixe as wel as I . . .
> For his honour, myself for to arraye.

and so she is driven to tell someone else:

> Thanne moot another payen for oure cost,
> Or lene us gold, and that is perilous.[1]

Perhaps the liveliest domestic scene is that between Chan-
ticleer and Pertelote, when with husbandly self-importance
he debates the prophetic meaning of a dream he has had
which his wife ascribes to constipation.

These are the variations on the theme proposed by the
Wife of Bath to which we return for a final statement by the
Franklin; his story voices that wise equability and kindliness
that is so great an attribute of Chaucer's mind. The *Franklin's*

[1] Lend us gold.

hero and heroine are married lovers; they had begun their attachment by falling in love in the best courtly manner:

> And many a labour, many a greet emprise[1]
> He for his lady wroghte, er she were wonne . . .
> . . . But atte last she, for his worthynesse,
> And namely[2] for his meke obeysaunce,
> Hath swich a pitee caught of his penaunce,
> That pryvely she fil of his accord
> To take hym for hir housbonde and hir lord.

This fourteenth-century Millamant and her Mirabell had, however, laid down certain provisos and counter-provisos before they agreed to marry; he was to exercise no 'maistrie' over her:

> But hire obeye, and folwe hir wyl in al

and she was to allow him 'the name of soveraynetee', so that he should not in public suffer the disgrace of his surrendered authority.

> That wolde he have for shame of his degree.

And, on this happy compromise, the *Franklin* stops his story for a moment to address the company with a Chaucerian wisdom suiting with his sanguine temperament:

> For o thyng, sires, saufly dar I seye,
> That freendes everych oother moot obeye,[3]
> If they wol longe holden compaignye.
> Love wol nat been constreyned by maistrye.
> Whan maistrie comth, the God of Love anon
> Beteth his wynges, and farewel, he is gon!
> Love is a thyng as any spirit free.
> Wommen, of kynde, desiren libertee[4]
> And nat to been constreyned as a thral;
> And so doon men, if I sooth seyen shal.

There was still one other ambient attitude to love-making in those times for Chaucer to voice and grace, namely the

[1] Enterprise.   [2] Especially.
[3] Friends must obey one another.   [4] Women, by nature, desire liberty.

attitude of the *fabliau*, the low-life oral tale of animal grab that in all ages circulates from mouth to mouth, like a limerick. In the typical *fabliau*, copulation seems to thrive in its cold-blooded way, borne along on strong undercurrents of guilt and hatred. Priests and Millers (the most powerful and therefore the most-to-be-humiliated men in the village) are generally the victims, and the very sexuality of the story, which, at one level, they are supposed to enjoy, at another level seems to be a part of their vileness, of their punishment, even. The laugh at the end is bitter with triumphant malice.

Chaucer took two such sows'-ear stories and turned them into the silk purses of *The Miller's Tale* and *The Reeve's Tale*. Here, at the bottom of the social scale, the clerical students of Oxford and Cambridge, happy-go-luckies of a saucy sexuality, are seen aping the adulteries of the aristocracy with all the cant of courtly love on their tongues. *Nicholas* in *The Miller's Tale* woos *Alison* with a—

> '. . . Lemman, love me al at ones,
> Or I wol dyen, also God me save!'

It is the argument that Pandarus uses on behalf of Troilus. *Absalom*, in the same story, goes on his knees (as Troilus did) to receive a kiss. That he got more than he bargained for cured him for ever, we are told, of love *par amour*, that is of courtly love. But Chaucer does more than this to rescue his *fabliaux* from their beastly dullness; the whole life of the village springs up before us, the rustic conversation, the superstition, the cunning; the impudence and bravado of the young in their gallantries, the rascality of the Miller, the gullibility of the Carpenter, the cottages they live in, and the vivid wenches:

> With buttokes brode, and brestes round and hye

of whose portraits Alison's is the most convincingly fresh and seductive that Chaucer, or anyone else, ever painted.

If, then, we ask ourselves what this 'servant of the servants of Love' knew about his masters, and about their Master, a short answer would be that he knew everything; everything that was known and felt on the subject at that time in Christendom. He voiced the whole thought of the Middle Ages, speaking as eloquently for Courtly as for Christian love, and as much an expert in marriage as in misogyny; everything came within the power of his pen, right down to the antics of John and Alan, Nicholas and Absalom and their 'popelotes'. No other English author has a comparable range in such matters. But it is not only a question of range, variety and subtlety in his art of love; it is the sympathy. He is all things to all men and women in all their moods and modes of love, able to write as easily of the lowest as of the highest:

> O mooder Mayde! O mayde Mooder free!
> O bussh unbrent, brennynge in Moyses sighte,
> That ravyshedest doun fro the Deitee,
> Thurgh thyn humblesse, the Goost that in th'alighte,
> Of whose vertu, whan he thyn herte lighte,
> Conceyved was the Fadres sapience . . .

(O bush unburnt, burning in the sight of Moses, thou that didst ravish down, from the Deity, the Spirit that alighted in thee, by thy humbleness; by whose power, when He illumined thy heart, the Sapience of the Father was conceived . . .)

The reason he can do so is that he takes joy in the created world, he grasps life affirmatively, and calls nothing that God has made unclean.

VI

MEN AND WOMEN

For the eye altering alters all
(William Blake: *The Mental Traveller*)

Chaucer thought the work of a writer to be something like that of a reaper, and it is with a wondering smile that we

hear him say that all the corn of poetry has been reaped
already and that only the gleanings are left for him after the
great poets have done their work:

> For wel I wot that folk han here-beforn
> Of makyng ropen, and lad awey the corn;[1]
> And I come after, glenynge here and there,
> And am ful glad if I may fynde en ere[2]
> Of any goodly word that they han left.
> > (*Prologue to the Legend of Good Women*)

The fields that he is thinking of are the fields of 'auctoritee'
that is, of the ancient writers that he loved so much, for their
poetry, philosophy and learning, whence all new learning
came:

> For out of olde feldes, as men seyth,
> Cometh al this newe corn from yer to yere,
> And out of olde bokes, in good feyth,
> Cometh al this newe science that men lere[3] . . .
> > (*The Parliament of Fowls*)

But there was another immense field, the field of Experience, which he himself was wont to contrast with
'Auctoritee'. It was the 'fair field full of folk' of which his
great contemporary, Langland, had written, the busy
London world of men and women, with whom, whether he
was at Court or in the Customs House, it was his profession
and his pleasure to deal.

No one had ever before looked at people in the way
Chaucer did; it was his eye that altered everything, it knew
what to look for. His was not only an observant, but an
instructed eye through which he looked out on to the world
of Experience. The instruction had, however, come to him
from Authority.

There are at least three kinds of book that we can observe

---

[1] For well I know that folk before now have reaped (the field of) poetry
and carried away the corn.   [2] Find an ear (of corn).   [3] Learn.

directing his discovery of human nature: books on *Rhetoric*, books on *Medicine*, and books on *Astrology*. From each of these he learnt something that helped to train his eye. To demonstrate this (as I shall now try) is not to offer an explanation of his genius, but *to show it at work*.

Other men may perhaps have known as much as he about rhetoric, medicine and astrology; but Chaucer knew how to use his knowledge, how to put his knowledge (so to speak) at the disposal of his eyes and ears. The result can be seen in the descriptions of the characters in the *Prologue* to *The Canterbury Tales*.

The Rhetoricians were perfectly clear on the subject of how to present a human being; it was a technique or figure known to them as *Descriptio*, of which there were at least three doctrines equally explicit, which were current in the Middle Ages. The first was Cicero's.

> Ac personis has res attributas putamus; nomen,
> naturam, victum, fotunam, habitum, affectionem,
> studia, consilia, facta, casus, orationes.
>
> (*De Inventione*, I. xxiv)
>
> (We hold the following to be the attributes of persons: name, nature, manner of life, fortune, habit, feeling, interests, purposes, achievements, accidents, conversation.)

As Cicero goes on to paraphrase these eleven attributes, we are able to gloss them, where necessary, as follows:

Name.

Nature. Includes Sex, place of origin, family, age, bodily appearance, whether bright or dull, affable or rude, patient or the reverse, and all qualities of mind or body bestowed by nature.

Manner of Life. Includes occupation, trade or profession and the character of the person's home-life.

Fortune. Includes whether rich or poor, successful or a failure, and rank.

Habit. Includes some special knowledge or bodily dexterity won by careful training and practice.

Feeling. A fleeting passion, such as joy, desire, fear, vexation, etc.

Interests. Mental activity devoted to some special subject.

Purposes. Any deliberate plan.

Achievements. What a person is doing, has done or will do.

Accidents. What is happening to a person, has happened, or will happen.

Conversation. What a person has said, is saying, or will say.

I suppose many readers will agree that the most strikingly described character in the *Prologue* is that of *The Wife of Bath*. In some thirty natural, easy lines of seemingly casual observation, she appears in startling completeness. For all that air of unconcern, Chaucer has worked his miracle by remembering his Cicero:

A good Wif was ther of biside Bathe	*Nature* (sex, place of origin)
But she was somdel deef, and that was scathe.	(bodily quality)
Of clooth-makying she hadde swich an haunt,	*Manner of Life* (trade)
She passed hem of Ypres and of Gaunt.	*Habit* (dexterity)
In al the parisshe wif ne was ther noon	*Fortune* (rank)
That to the offrynge bifore hire sholde goon;	
And if ther dide, certeyne so wrooth was she,	*Feeling* (vexation)
That she was out of alle charitee.	
Hir coverchiefs ful fyne weren of ground;	*Nature* (appearance)
I dorste swere they weyeden ten pound	
That on a Sonday weren upon hir heed.	
Hir hosen weren of fyn scarlet reed,	
Ful streite yteyd, and shoes ful moyste and newe.	
Boold was hir face and fair, and reed of hewe.	
She was a worthy womman al hir lyve:	*Fortune* (rank)
Housbondes at chirche dore she hadde fyve,	*Manner of Life* (home-life)
Withouten oother compaignye in youthe—	

But thereof nedeth nat to speke as nowthe.	(*Occupation*)
And thries had she been at Jerusalem;	*Achievements* (past doings)
She hadde passed many a straunge strem;	and *Accidents*
At Rome she hadde been, and at Boloigne,	
In Galice at Seint Jame, and at Coloigne.	
She koude muchel of wandrynge by the weye.	*Habit* (special knowledge)
Gat-tothed was she, soothly for to seye.	*Nature* (bodily quality)
Upon an amblere esily she sat,	*Achievements* (what doing)
Ywympled wel, and on hir head an hat	*Nature* (appearance)
As brood as is a bokeler or a targe;	
A foot-mantel aboute hir hippes large,	
And on hir feet a paire of spores sharpe.	
In felaweshipe wel koude she laughe and carpe.	*Conversation*
Of remedies of love she knew per chaunce.	*Interests*
For she koude of that art the olde daunce.	

The only points demanded by Cicero that are left out are her name and purposes. We learn later that her name was Alison; as for her purposes, one of them could go without saying—to seek the shrine of St. Thomas with the other pilgrims. We may perhaps infer another:

> Yblessed be God that I have wedded fyve!
> Welcome the sixte, whan that evere he shal.
>
> (*Prologue* to her *Tale*)

Ciceronian as is her portrait, Cicero cannot claim it all. There is the hint of something learnt from Geoffrey de Vinsauf in it too. De Vinsauf's teaching was that a description must start at the top of the head and inch its way downwards, detail by detail, to the feet—*poliatur ad unguem*, let it be polished to the toe-nail. To follow this counsel slavishly would lead to what, in another context, Chaucer calls the 'fulsomness of his prolixitee'; but he follows it selectively, beginning with the ten-pound head-dress. His eye is then drawn for an instant from the boldness of her face to her all-too-striking hose, but returns to her face and wimple, glides to her hips and falls to her spurs.

A third doctrine of *Descriptio* was that of Matthieu de Vendôme, who held that a writer must first describe the moral nature and then the physical appearance of his subject. Chaucer moved easily among all these prescriptions, allowing each to point in some direction where the discerning eye could pause, the attentive ear listen. So it comes about that the account of the *Prioress* in *The Prologue* begins in the Ciceronian manner (name, sex, profession, social position, special skill and her prevailing study, 'to been estatlich of manere'), then follows Matthieu with an account of her moral sensibilities, her amiable carriage, her charity and tenderness of heart, her charming sentimentality over her pets (which, as a nun, she had of course no business to own), and at last comes to her appearance; here he follows Vinsauf, starting with her wimple and thence to nose, eyes and mouth, moving downward to the tell-tale wrist with its ambiguous brooch, inscribed *Amor Vincit Omnia*. Her portrait is a perfect example of how rules obey a genius.

There was also a medical approach to character. Medicine had evolved a theory that the human constitution was fashioned of the Four Elements, earth, air, fire and water. *Earth* had the quality of being cold and dry: *air*, hot and moist: *fire*, hot and dry: *water*, cold and moist. Now according to the particular proportion and mixture of these elements in the individual man, he was thought to have a predominating 'complexion' or temperament. Too earthy he would be *melancholy:* too airy, he would be *sanguine:* too fiery, he would be *choleric:* too watery, he would be *phlegmatic.*

To each of these 'complexions' or 'humours' were attached a number of subsidiary qualities and predispositions, so well known as to be enshrined in popular mnemonic verses, Latin and English. Here, for instance, is a popular rhyme to remind you what to expect of a *Sanguine* man:

> Of yiftes large,[1] in love hath grete delite,
> Iocunde and gladde, ay of laughyng chiere,
> Of ruddy colour meynt somdel with white;[2]
> Disposed by kynde to be a champioun,[3]
> Hardy I-nough, manly, and bold of chiere.
>   Of the sangwyne also it is a signe
>   To be demure, right curteys, and benynge.
>   (Robbins, *Secular Lyrics of the 14th and 15th centuries*)

The Prologue tells us that the *Franklin* was a sanguine man, and that one word is intended to carry all the qualities listed in the rhyme. They fit him very well, not only as we first see him, but as we see him later on during his colloquy with the *Squire*, and in the tenor of his tale. The *Reeve*, we are told, was a choleric; all that he says and does is in keeping with what medical lore asserted of such men, who were held to be refractory, deceitful, given to anger, full of ruses, lustful, hardy, small and slender, dry of nature, covetous and solemn. Indeed the Host rebukes him for solemnity in the prelude to his tale. The *Pardoner's* moral and physical nature are described in terms from which any Doctor (as Professor Curry has made clear) could at once have diagnosed him as a eunuch from birth, and this fact about him explains much in his subsequent adventures on the pilgrimage. Chaucer helped himself to medical lore in much the way a modern novelist might use his knowledge of Freud or Jung.

Astrology offered yet another approach to the imagining of a character. Professor Curry has also shown that the characters of King Emetrius and King Lycurgus in *The Knight's Tale* are imagined as 'personal representatives, in the lists, of the astrological forces' that are involved in the story, namely of Saturn and of Mars respectively, and he quotes Claudius Ptolemaeus to show that the description of

---

[1] Large in his giving.   [2] Mingled somewhat with white.
[3] Disposed by nature.

these kings by Chaucer follows almost exactly the physical details attributed to men born under those planets. Horoscopy is explicitly invoked by the *Wife of Bath* to account for the contradictions in her character; they were dictated by the position of the heavenly bodies at her birth:

> For certes, I am al Venerien
> In feelynge, and myn herte is Marcien.
> Venus me yaf my lust, my likerousnesse,
> And Mars yaf me my sturdy hardynesse;
> Myn ascendent was Taur, and Mars therinne.
> Allas, allas, that ever love was synne!

Instructed in such ways as these by *auctoritee*, Chaucer looked out with sharpened eyes upon *experience*, and saw not only how to grasp the essentials of a personality posed for a portrait, but also how to make use of what is latent in other ways within a given personality and to draw it forth with a surprising touch of individual or local colour. For instance, in *The Miller's Tale* one of the characters is a super-stitious old carpenter, living at Osney, just outside Oxford. When, peeping into the room of his lodger, Nicholas, to find out what is wrong with him, he sees Nicholas lying gaping on his back on the floor:

> This carpenter to blessen hym bigan,
> And seyde 'Help us, seinte Frydeswyde!'

In other words, he crossed himself and invoked St. Frides-wide, the local Oxford Saint. One could tell that the carpenter was an Oxford man, simply from that.

In like manner, in *The Reeve's Tale*, the Miller's wife, awoken by the battle between Alan and the Miller, and feeling the sudden weight of her husband's body falling on top of her, cries out:

> 'Help! hooly croys of Bromeholm!'

This relic, the Holy Cross of Bromeholm, was preserved in East Norfolk, where the Reeve came from, not very far from Cambridge, where the Miller's wife lived. No one else in

Chaucer invokes St. Frideswide or the Cross of Bromeholm; they are pin-points of local colour, latent in the people he was creating, and perceived by him.

This power of seeing the implications in a character or a situation, so as to give a sudden twist or flavour, depth or tone to his tale, is one of the important things that make Chaucer immeasurably superior as a story-teller to his friend and contemporary John Gower, and indeed to all writers of English narrative poetry. The perceptiveness of which I am speaking is continuously, sensitively, present throughout *Troilus & Criseyde*, in which there is never a false move or impulse of feeling, and the whole is sensed to be deploying humanly, freely, and yet inevitably, under the compulsions latent in the characters, in their struggle with destiny.

On a smaller scale, we may see the operation of this kind of insight in *The Merchant's Tale*, perhaps his most masterly short story. It is characterized by Chaucer's usual moral lucidity. Nothing could be clearer than the never-stated motive of rebellious lust present in its three main characters. These are Old January, whose senile sexuality is hallowed by matrimony and encouraged by aphrodisiacs; young Damian with his treacherous animalism; and the 'faire fresshe May' who is ready to climb a tree for it.

With rarest comment by the narrator, all three are presented through their own eyes, that is, with all the sympathy and self-approval that they all separately feel for the fantasy-lives latent within them, which Chaucer elicits. January sees himself as a dear, kind, wise old gentleman, penitent for his past, eager to sin no more, and seeking the delicious safety and sanctity of wedlock; his earnest care in consulting his friends in the choice of a wife (but insisting that she be under twenty), his tender apprehensions lest she be too delicate to endure his amorous heats, his solicitude for the sick squire Damian (who is about to cuckold him) and for his wife's soul (about to collaborate with the squire), are all presented from the old man's point of view; in his own opinion, he is a generous, romantic figure; his wife will wear mourning

for ever after his death. We even hear his doting use of
troubadour-language to entice his wife into the Priapic
Garden of the Rose which he had designed for their summery
encounters; like Absalom and Nicholas, he would be a
courtly lover too:

> 'Rys up, my wyf, my love, my lady free!
> The turtles voys is herd, my dowve sweete;
> The wynter is goon with alle his reynes weete.
> Com forth now, with thyne eyen columbyn,[1]
> How fairer been thy brestes than is wyn! . . .

At the end of this dithyramb, Chaucer (or his *persona*, the
Merchant) permits himself the remark:

> Swiche olde lewed wordes used he.

But the irony does not consist in the bare contrast between
this fantasy of courtly love and the nastiness of the old lecher
who utters it; he is nothing so simple as a rich, dirty old man;
perhaps no one is. He *is* considerate, affectionate and
generous—humble, even ready to admit his dislikable
qualities to his girl-wife:

> '. . . And though that I be jalous, wyte me noght.[2]
> Ye been so depe enprented in my thoght,
> That, whan I considere youre beautee,
> And therwithal the unlikely elde of me,[6]
> I may not, certes, though I sholde dye,
> Forbere to been out of youre compaignye
> For verray love; this is withouten doute.
> Now kys me, wyf, and lat us rome aboute.'

In all the irony, there is pathos; and in the pathos, irony.
That January should go blind (as he does in the course of the
story) is pathetic, but it is ironic, too. He had been blind all
along.

> O Januarie, what myghte it thee availle,
> Thogh thou myghte se as fer as shippes saille?

[1] With thy dove's eyes.   [2] Blame me not.   [3] My dislikable old age.

> For as good is blind deceyved be
> As to be deceyved whan a man may se.[1]

In like manner, young Damian, the seducer, is, in his own esteem, a lover-poet; he wears the verses that he writes to May in a silk purse upon his heart, and May, who reads and memorizes his lines in a lavatory (to which, for safety, she consigns them) is a heroine of romance to herself:

> 'Certeyn,' thoghte she, 'whom that this thyng displese,
> I rekke noght, for heere I hym assure
> To love hym best of any creature,
> Though he namoore hadde than his sherte!'

Again the ironical narrator allows himself to intrude:

> Lo, pitee renneth soone in gentil herte!

No moral is pointed at the end of this story; by a perfection of irony, they all lived happily ever after.

There is one character in Chaucer that neither realistic observation nor the authority of ancient books can wholly account for. He comes from some unknown half-world, a visiting presence that some have thought to be the figure of Death, some the Wandering Jew, some the Old Adam, seeking renewal. It may be better to leave him wholly mysterious and unexplained; it is the ancient, muffled man who directs the three rioters of *The Pardoner's Tale* to the heap of gold, when they ask him if he knows where Death is to be found. To their rough language, and the question why he is so old, he gives this strange reply:

> 'For I ne kan nat fynde
> A man, though that I walked into Ynde,
> Neither in citee ne in no village,
> That wolde chaunge his youthe for myn age;
> And therefore moot I han myn age stille,
> As longe tyme as it is Goddes wille.

[1] For it is as good to be deceived when blind as when you have your sight.

Ne Deeth, allas! ne wol nat han my lyf.
'Thus walke I, lyk a restelees kaityf,[1]
And on the ground, which is my moodres gate,
I knokke with my staf, bothe erly and late,
And seye 'Leeve mooder, leet me in!
Lo how I vanysshe, flessh, and blood, and skyn!
Allas! whan shul my bones been at rest? . . .'

It is an unexpected shock to meet with so haunting a figure
in the bright Chaucerian world, a figure so loaded with
suggestions of supernatural meaning. With slow gravity, he
rebukes the three rioters for their discourteous behaviour:

'But, sires, to yow it is no curteisye
To speken to an old man vileynye.'

and that is the reader's link with this strange phantom and
the shadowy world to which he belongs—the huge importance of courtesy. We are never told who our instructor is,
nor has he been found in any book that Chaucer studied,
save for a few hints in the obscure Latin poet Maximian; the
essential creation is all Chaucer's and it was his 'cyclopean
eye' that discerned this eerie figure, tap-tapping his invisible
way through the crowds at Queenshithe or by the Custom
House, and among the courtiers of Richard II at the palaces
of Eltham or of Shene.

VII

ENVOY

'. . . I am sure you are become a good Chaucerist . . .'
(Ralph Winwood, in a letter to
Sir Thomas Edmondes, 1601)

I have tried to present Chaucer's career as a courtier and to
suggest its effect on his career as a poet, rather than write an
all-embracing 'honeysuckle life'. If this approach leaves

[1] Like a restless captive.

much unsaid that needs saying, there are many other studies to supply my deficiences. More can always be said of any great poet.

His greatness has been a little impugned by Matthew Arnold, in a celebrated passage, where Chaucer is accused of lacking 'high seriousness'. It is clear, however, that Arnold knew very little about Chaucer; he only shows a slight acquaintance with *The Canterbury Tales* and does not appear to have read *Troilus & Criseyde* at all. It need not, therefore, surprise us that he did not perceive Chaucer's moral stature, or that he could not find high seriousness in high comedy; he did not know where to look for it.

There is so much fun in Chaucer, and so little reproof, that his appeal to moralists (who are seldom quite happy about pleasure) is not immediate. Yet he is one of those rare poets who can strongly affect, not only our passions and intelligence, but our wills too; he creates generosities in them. A sense of welcome to the created world, to men and women, and to the experience of living, flows from his pen.

He can reach out to a supernal world too; and if, to do so, he has borrowed a little from Dante, he knew what to borrow and how to borrow it:

> Thow oon, and two, and thre, eterne on lyve,
> That regnest ay in thre, and two, and oon,
> Uncircumscript, and al maise circumscrive,
> Us, from visible and invisible foon,
> Defende . . .

(Troilus & Criseyde, V)

(Thou one and Two and Three, that livest eternally and reignest ever in Three and Two and One, uncomprehended, and yet comprehending all things, defend us from visible and invisible foes . . .)

or

> Withinne the cloistre blisful of thy sydis
> Took mannes shap the eterneel love and pees.

(Second Nun's Prologue)

(Within the blissful cloister of thy womb, the eternal love and peace took human shape.)

Victorious tree, proteccioun of trewe,
That oonly worthy were for to bere
The Kyng of Hevene with his woundes newe,
The white Lamb that hurt was with a spere . . .

(Victorious Tree, the protection of all true (souls), that alone
wert worthy to bear the King of Heaven . . .)

(*Man of Law's Tale*)

But it is the mortal world that most exercised his poetical
gift, and there he is nearest to Shakespeare as the poet of
humane understanding; like him, he begets a *caritas* in the
imagination of his readers. His vision of earth ranges from
one of amused delight to one of grave compassion; these are
his dawn and his dusk. His daylight is a lively April of fresh
good will and kindly common sense, and if, here and there,
there is a delicate frost of irony, warmth is his great charac-
teristic. He takes deep joy in what we think of as the simple
things of nature—birdsong, sunlight, gardens, daisies in the
grass, the 'ayerissh bestes' of the sky (the ram, the bull and
other signs of the zodiac zoo) and even in a chance, timid
hound-puppy:

And as I wente, ther cam by mee
A whelp, that fauned me as I stood,
That hadde yfolowed, and koude no good.
Hyt com and crepte to me as lowe
Rhyte as hyt hadde me yknowe,
Helde doun hys hed and joyned hys eres,
And leyde al smothe doun hys heres;
I wolde have kaught hyt, and anoon
Hyt fledde, and was from me goon . . .

(*The Book of the Duchess*)

The joy he seems to experience, he can communicate, or
create in others, and that is to create a kind of goodness, or a
mood that makes goodness easier; he forges a basic sense of
and desire for harmony. His universe is not off-course, but
on the way to a perhaps distant but a happy and Christian
fulfilment, in which men and women have their generous

share. There are plenty of rascals among them, to be sure; he gazes at them evenly with unembarrassed, uncondemning delight, limiting his aspirations to *tout comprendre*, and leaving *tout pardonner* to Higher Authority.

All this is done with laughter not left behind, nor music either. If Matthew Arnold was a little blind where Chaucer was concerned, at least he was not deaf, and has written with wonderful discernment and eloquence on the sound of Chaucer's verses:

> . . . of Chaucer's divine liquidness of diction, of his divine fluidity of movement, it is difficult to speak temperately. They are irresistible, and justify all the rapture with which his successors speak of his 'gold dew-drops of speech' . . .

Chaucer's music was not unrelated to that courtiership of his that we have been studying. The *Liber Niger* of Edward IV ordains that young henxmen shall be encouraged to 'harping, to pype and sing'. Squires of his household—

> of old be accustomed, winter and summer, in afternoons and evenings, to draw to Lordes Chambres within Court, there to keep honest company after there Cunninge, in talking of Cronicles of Kinges and other Pollicies, or in pipeing or harpeing, songinges and other actes marcealls, to helpe to occupie the Court, and accompanie estrangers . . .

In afternoons and evenings, Chaucer's music would be heard in his own voice (after his cunning), when he read out his poems. In winter, in a Lord's chamber, or in the great hall; in summer, in the garden below, where he would 'help to occupie the Court' and 'accompanie estrangers', Jean Froissart, perhaps, among the others.

The College of Corpus Christi, Cambridge, owns a fifteenth-century manuscript of *Troilus & Criseyde;* in this there is a full-page illumination of just such a scene. Against a sky of afternoon gold, rise the trees and towers of a royal palace, Shene, it may be, or Windsor, or Eltham; a company of young lords and ladies in the richly simple robes of those times are moving down the garden slopes towards a dell, where a small pulpit has been set up. It is surrounded by the gathering Court: the Queen is seated on the grass before it, with her ladies about her. King Richard stands in cloth of gold, a little to the left of her; to the right there stands an older man in blue, with a gold girdle. It might be John of Gaunt. In the pulpit, at which this older man is gazing, Geoffrey Chaucer is reading from a book; he seems to be a youngish man, his face not unlike that in the picture which fronts this essay, but the hair and the eyes are brown; young as they are, they have something of the same sad look.

He is reading from his greatest completed poem, the first tragedy in our language, *Troilus & Criseyde*:

> Go, litel bok, go, litel myn tragedye,
> Ther God thi makere yet, er that he dye,
> So sende myght to make in som comedye!
> But litel bok, no makyng thow n'envie,
> But subgit be to alle poesye;
> And kis the steppes, where as thow seest pace
> Virgile, Ovide, Omer, Lucan and Stace.

The 'litel bok' did its errand and the 'myght' was duly sent him; it gave us our first and freshest comedy, *The Canterbury Tales*.

(Go, little book, go my little tragedy, to that place whence may God likewise yet send thy maker power to make something in the manner of a comedy, before he dies! But, little book, envy no other poetry, but be subject to all poesy, and kiss the steps where thou seest Virgil, Ovid, Homer, Lucan and Statius pacing.)

GEOFFREY CHAUCER

Select Bibliography

BIBLIOGRAPHIES AND REFERENCE WORKS

HAMMOND, ELEANOR P. *Chaucer: A Bibliographical Manual.* New York: Macmillan, 1908.

GRIFFITH, DUDLEY D. *Bibliography of Chaucer 1908–1953.* University of Washington Publications in Language and Literature Volume 13. Seattle: University of Washington Press, 1955.
A continuation of the previous item. Includes the contents of Griffith's *A Bibliography of Chaucer 1908–1924* (1926).

SPURGEON, CAROLINE F. *Five Hundred Years of Chaucer Criticism and Allusion, 1357–1900.* 3 vols. Cambridge: University Press, 1925; New York: Russell and Russell, 1960.

TATLOCK, JOHN S. P., AND ARTHUR G. KENNEDY. *A Concordance to the Complete Works of Geoffrey Chaucer and to the Romaunt of the Rose.* Carnegie Institution of Washington, 1927.

FRENCH, ROBERT DUDLEY. *A Chaucer Handbook.* New York: F. S. Crofts, 1927; 2nd ed. New York: Appleton-Century-Crofts, 1947.

MAGOUN, FRANCIS P. *A Chaucer Gazetteer.* Chicago: University of Chicago Press, 1961.

BRYAN, WILLIAM F., AND GERMAINE DEMPSTER, eds. *Sources and Analogues of Chaucer's Canterbury Tales.* Chicago: University of Chicago Press, 1941.

GORDON, ROBERT K., ed. *The Story of Troilus as Told by Benoît de Sainte-Maure, Giovanni Boccaccio, Geoffrey Chaucer, and Robert Henryson.* London: Dent, 1934.

KÖKERITZ, HELGE. *A Guide to Chaucer's Pronunciation.* New York: Holt, Rinehart and Winston, 1962.

EDITIONS

The Complete Works of Geoffrey Chaucer. Edited by Walter W. Skeat.

6 vols. Oxford: Clarendon Press, 1894. A seventh volume of "Chaucerian and Other Pieces," 1897.
The fullest edition.

The Works of Geoffrey Chaucer. Edited by Fred N. Robinson. Boston: Houghton Mifflin, 1933. 2nd ed., 1957.
A complete edition in one volume. The full notes and citations summarize very compactly Chaucer scholarship until about 1955, with an emphasis on the historical approach. The glossary is generalized and not too helpful. The standard edition.

Chaucer's Poetry: An Anthology for the Modern Reader. Selected and edited by E. Talbot Donaldson. New York: Ronald Press, 1958.
Omits, among others, the *Romance of the Rose, The Friar's Tale, The Parson's Tale.* Regularized (not modernized) spelling, with glosses at the foot of the page. With a fresh critical (not historical) commentary, and no citations.

Chaucer's Major Poetry. Edited by Albert C. Baugh. New York: Appleton-Century-Crofts, 1963.
Omits the *Romance of the Rose, The Parson's Tale,* and others. Glosses at the foot of the page. With a brief historical commentary and citations.

The Text of the Canterbury Tales. Edited by John M. Manly and Edith Rickert. 8 vols. Chicago: University of Chicago Press, 1940.
Edited and studied on the basis of all the numerous known manuscripts.

The Book of Troilus and Criseyde. Edited by Robert Kilburn Root. Princeton: Princeton University Press, 1926.
Standard edition.

The Equatorie of the Planetis. Edited by Derek J. Price. Cambridge: University Press, 1955.
A newly edited astrological work, conjecturally ascribed to Chaucer.

TRANSLATIONS OF CHAUCER

Of the many attempts to translate Chaucer, the following are convenient, full—or nearly full—and recent.

The Canterbury Tales. Translated by Robert M. Lumiansky. New York: Simon and Schuster, 1948.
In prose. Contains also some of the Middle English text.

The Canterbury Tales. Translated by Nevill Coghill. Baltimore: Penguin Books, 1952.
In verse. Frequently reprinted.

Troilus and Cressida. Translated by George Philip Krapp. New York: Random House, 1932.
In verse.

Troilus and Criseyde. Translated by Robert M. Lumiansky. Columbia, S.C.: University of South Carolina Press, 1952.
In prose, with some of the Middle English text.

BIOGRAPHICAL AND CRITICAL STUDIES OF CHAUCER

LOUNSBURY, THOMAS R. *Studies in Chaucer.* 3 vols. New York: Harper and Brothers, 1892; Russell and Russell, 1962.

COULTON, GEORGE GORDON. *Chaucer and His England.* New York: Putnam, 1908; 8th ed. New York: Dutton, 1950; Barnes and Noble, 1963.

LEGOUIS, ÉMILE. *Geoffrey Chaucer.* Les Grandes Écrivains Étrangers. Paris: Bloud, 1910.
Translated by L. Lailavoix (New York: Dutton, 1913; Russell and Russell, 1961).

KITTREDGE, GEORGE LYMAN. *Chaucer and his Poetry.* Cambridge: Harvard University Press, 1915.
Frequently reprinted.

BRUSENDORF, AAGE. *The Chaucer Tradition.* London: Oxford University Press, 1925.

CURRY, WALTER CLYDE. *Chaucer and the Mediaeval Sciences.* New York: Oxford University Press, 1926; 2nd ed. rev. and enlarged, New York: Barnes and Noble, 1960.

MANLY, JOHN M. *Some New Light on Chaucer.* New York: Henry Holt, 1926; P. Smith, 1952.

———. *Chaucer and the Rhetoricians.* The British Academy Warton Lecture on English Poetry No. XVII. London: Oxford University Press, 1926.

COWLING, GEORGE H. *Chaucer.* New York: Dutton, 1927.

LOWES, JOHN LIVINGSTON. *The Art of Geoffrey Chaucer.* Sir Israel Gollancz Memorial Lecture, British Academy, 1930. New York: Oxford University Press, 1931.

———. *Geoffrey Chaucer and the Development of his Genius.* Boston: Houghton Mifflin, 1934; Bloomington: Indiana University Press, 1958.

WHITING, BARTLETT J. *Chaucer's Use of Proverbs*. Harvard Studies in Comparative Philology and Literature No. 11. Cambridge: Harvard University Press, 1934.

CHUTE, MARCHETTE. *Geoffrey Chaucer of England*. New York: Dutton, 1946.

BENNETT, H. S. *Chaucer and the Fifteenth Century*. The Oxford History of English Literature Vol. II. Oxford: Clarendon Press, 1947.

BOWDEN, MURIEL. *A Commentary on the General Prologue to the Canterbury Tales*. New York: Macmillan, 1948.

RICKERT, EDITH. *Chaucer's World*. Edited by Clair Olson and Martin Crow. New York: Columbia University Press, 1948; and 1962.

COGHILL, NEVILL. *The Poet Chaucer*. The Home University of Modern Knowledge No. 185. London and New York: Oxford University Press, 1949.

LAWRENCE, WILLIAM W. *Chaucer and the Canterbury Tales*. New York: Columbia University Press, 1950.

MALONE, KEMP. *Chapters on Chaucer*. Baltimore: The Johns Hopkins Press, 1951.

SPEIRS, JOHN. *Chaucer the Maker*. London: Faber and Faber, 1951. 2nd ed. 1960.

LUMIANSKY, ROBERT M. *Of Sondry Folk: The Dramatic Principle in the Canterbury Tales*. Austin: University of Texas Press, 1955.

MUSCATINE, CHARLES. *Chaucer and the French Tradition*. Berkeley: University of California Press, 1957.

WAGENKNECHT, EDWARD, ed. *Chaucer: Modern Essays in Criticism*. A Galaxy Book. New York: Oxford University Press, 1959.

BRONSON, BERTRAND H. *In Search of Chaucer*. Toronto: University of Toronto Press, 1960.

SCHOECK, RICHARD J., AND JEROME TAYLOR, eds. *Chaucer Criticism*. 2 vols. Notre Dame: University of Notre Dame Press, 1960–1962.
Selected criticism. Vol. I, *The Canterbury Tales;* Vol. II, *Troilus and Cressida* and minor poems.

OWENS, CHARLES, ed. *Discussions of the Canterbury Tales*. Boston: D. C. Heath, 1961.
Selected criticism.

BROOKS, HAROLD F. *Chaucer's Pilgrims: The Artistic Order of the Portraits in the Prologue*. New York: Barnes and Noble, 1962.

HUPPÉ, BERNARD F., AND D. W. ROBERTSON, JR. *Fruyt and Chaf: Studies in Chaucer's Allegories*. Princeton: Princeton University Press, 1963.

RECORDINGS

The Canterbury Tales: The General Prologue. Read in Middle English by J. B. Bessinger. Caedmon–TC 1151.

The Canterbury Tales: The Pardoner's Tale and The Nun's Priest's Tale. Read in Middle English by Robert Ross. Caedmon–TC 1008.

The Canterbury Tales: The Wife of Bath's Prologue and Tale. Read in Modern English by Dame Peggy Ashcroft. Caedmon–TC 1102.

The Canterbury Tales: Selections. Read in Modern English (Nevill Coghill's modernization) by B.B.C. performers, with some passages read in Middle English. The Spoken Word–101/4.

Includes *The General Prologue, The Nun's Priest's Tale, The Reve's Tale, The Manciple's Tale,* and others.

Chaucer Readings. Read in Middle English by Helge Kökeritz. Lexington–5505.

Selections from *The Canterbury Tales* and *Troilus and Criseyde*.

SIR THOMAS MALORY

by M. C. Bradbrook

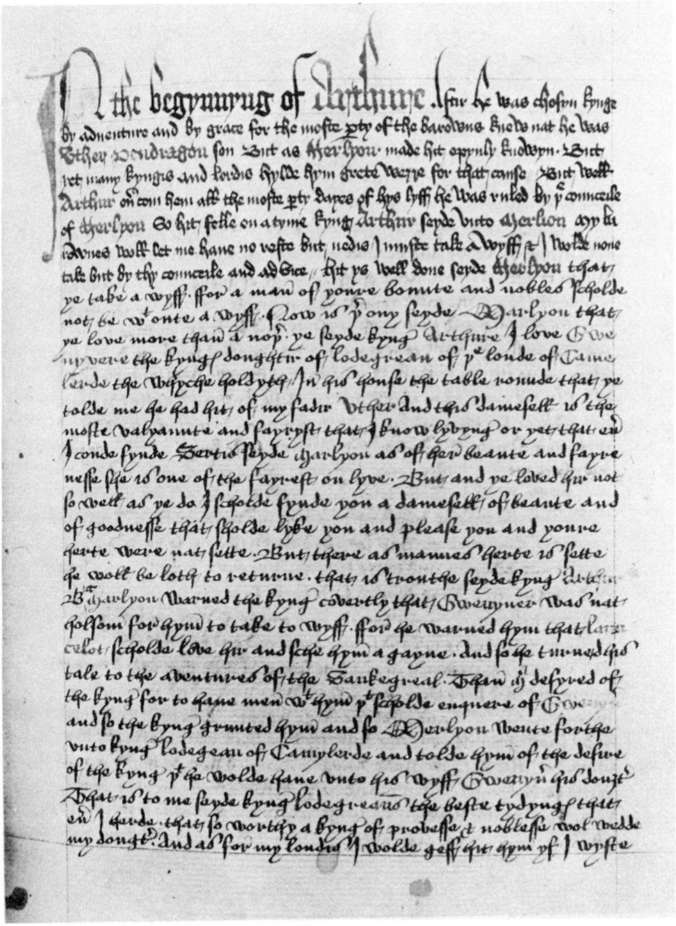

¶ SIR THOMAS MALORY was born of a Warwickshire family, early in the fifteenth century. He died in 1471.

I

THE KNIGHT PRISONER

W. B. Yeats kept in his study a scrap of silk from a Japanese lady's dress, and a Samurai sword, as

> things that are
> Emblematic of love and war.

These two themes are fundamental to the work of Sir Thomas Malory. Religion—the third of the great epic themes—is admittedly and nobly subordinated; only at the end, Guinevere, in expiation of her guilt in destroying the Round Table, becomes a nun; and Lancelot, for love of her and not for love of God, takes on himself the habit of perfection.

For nearly five hundred years, since its publication from William Caxton's printing press at Westminster on 31 July 1485, Malory's *Morte Darthur* has stood at the centre of English literature. It has been read, and it has nourished the work of other writers, but it has been little discussed. This is, in fact, one of the silent areas in English criticism, and (like the silent areas in the brain) such deceptively simple works, which offer nothing to be clever about, are the centres of high creative activity. Spenser's debt to Malory is clear; throughout the nineteenth century he was used as quarry, and for the poetry of Tennyson and the Pre-Raphaelites he provided an essential basis; in our own day, T. S. Eliot has described Malory as one of his favourite authors. Chaucer in the fourteenth century and Malory in the fifteenth together laid the foundations of modern English narrative; the scale of their work as well as its excellence, its breadth combined with its individuality, established and fortified the art of the imaginative story, in poetry and in prose. They are the only two English medieval writers who have been continuously and widely known from their own day to this.

The differences between them are more obvious than

the likeness. Chaucer, a diplomat and civil servant, writing for the elegant and sophisticated court of Richard II, with a cosmopolitan taste and a fine tact, a delicate malice and a most urbane wit, might have felt there was some rusticity, some touch of 'rim, ram, ruf' about Malory, who did in fact begin his work by turning into prose an alliterative English poem of the fourteenth century, of the kind which Chaucer would certainly have thought exceedingly provincial. In *The Canterbury Tales*, it is the middle-class Wyf of Bath who tells an Arthurian fairy story, while Chaucer burlesques the whole tradition of Romance in the delicious *Tale of Sir Thopas*, which he gives to himself to tell in his role of boring and incompetent simpleton. This is, of course, a burlesque of the popular and not of the courtly Romance; but it suggests that in Chaucer's mind tales of wandering knights had already turned into Old Wives' Tales.

Malory belonged to the next age, that turbulent fifteenth century whose disorder Shakespeare depicted in the trilogy of *Henry VI*, where the civil strife of the Wars of the Roses culminates with the scene of a lamenting king set between a son who has killed his father and a father who has killed his son. Whether the Wars of the Roses were really disastrous for any but the small class of barons and knights is very problematic; but it was just this class, the remnants of an earlier society, from which Malory sprang, and which is idealized in the Table Round. Malory belonged to that older order of chivalry which finally went down on Bosworth Field in 1485, the year in which his work was published, fourteen years after his own death on 14 March 1471.

Sir Thomas Malory came from Shakespeare's county of Warwickshire, and his family estate was at Newbold Revell. As a young man, in 1436 he served in the train of the great Richard Beauchamp, Earl of Warwick. Later he entered Parliament. But such records as survive of Malory's middle years show the depressing picture of an old fighter turned gangster. He stole cattle and does; broke into an

abbey; robbed under threats of violence; and even planned
to ambush and murder the Duke of Buckingham. His one
recorded amorous exploit is the felonious ravishing of
Joan, wife of Henry Smyth, of Monks' Kirby, near Newbold
Revell. All these events took place within some eighteen
months of each other in 1450–1. Twice he broke jail,
once by swimming the castle moat at Coleshill and once
by fighting his way out at Colchester. So began his career
of imprisonment, punctuated by spells of freedom, in
which he later developed a taste for horse-stealing. He was
imprisoned again, released again, and even returned to
Parliament in 1456. Imprisoned yet again, and yet again
set free; seen now with the Yorkists, but afterwards following Richard Neville, Earl of Warwick, it would seem, in
his desertion to the Lancastrians, Malory was in 1468 twice
excluded from general pardons granted by Edward IV.
His death in 1471 must have come when he was about
sixty, and some two years after he had finished the *Morte
Darthur* in 'the ninth year of the reign of King Edward
the Fourth' as he tells in the colophon. He was buried in
London, in the church of the Grey Friars near to Newgate,
having tasted in his time most of the London prisons,
including the Tower.

Fortune's wheel whirled Malory continually lower and
lower, in contrast to successful climbers like the Paston
family, whose Letters show them rising in the social scale
throughout the fifteenth century by methods sometimes
as violent as Malory's but more skilfully timed. The landless
knight, the man-at-arms who followed his lord to foreign
wars, inevitably turned to violence when loosed upon his
native soil, as the disbanded soldier took to begging or
highway robbery; though Malory himself was not landless,
he behaved as one of this class, and some of his imprison-
ments were for debt. His story of violence, disaster and
stormy veerings to and fro may seem at variance with the
modern notions of chivalry; but Malory seems to have
retained the first chivalric virtue, that of loyalty to his lord.

Here, however, his allegiance illustrates once more the decline of chivalry. Richard Beauchamp, Earl of Warwick, whom he followed as a young man to Calais, was a pattern of courtesy as well as a great lord. Richard Neville, the Kingmaker, who succeeded to the title after his marriage to Beauchamp's granddaughter, and who made and unmade kings in Malory's later years, was the father of a queen, and himself greater than a king in possessions; but his rapid changes of party, his merciless slaughter of conquered enemies, above all his unnatural position of superiority and domination towards his lord the King seem to epitomize all that Malory and later even Shakespeare dreaded as the supreme evil of evil times—the dissolution of harmony, order and degree which a divided rule may bring.

Malory wrote his work in prison. At the end of *The Tale of King Arthur*, standing first in the book, the Winchester MS. has a note that it was written 'by a knight prisoner, Sir Thomas Malleorré, that God send him good recover'. At the end of the *Tale of Sir Gareth*, the writer appeals:

> And I pray you all that readeth this tale to pray for him that this wrote, that God send him good deliverance soon and hastily. Amen.

At the end of Caxton's printed version comes the paragraph entreating all gentlemen and gentlewomen 'pray for me while I am on live that God send me good deliverance. And when I am dead, I pray you all pray for my soul'; the writer himself adds such a prayer '. . . by Sir Thomas Maleoré knight as Jesu help him for His great might, as he is the servant of Jesu both day and night'. This piteous little jingle suggests that by the ninth year of the reign of King Edward IV Malory had lost hope in an earthly deliverance.

Those who have seen the works of art produced by prisoners of war—the elaborate frigates carved out of meat-bones in the Napoleonic Wars, the stone cross which Colonel Carne of the Gloucester Regiment chipped out with a nail during his solitary confinement in Korea—will not be surprised at the immense care and pains which are shown in *Le Morte Darthur* by the development of the style. Painfully and slowly Malory evolved his own prose, learnt an eloquence, a craftsmanship and a power of organization which could not have come easily to one who was not a clerk. He had all the time in the world in which to learn.

THE KNIGHTLY ROMANCE

Story-telling was the great art of the Middle Ages, and the Romance was a special form of this art. It was a long-continuing and popular form; the stories which Malory told were also in substance many hundreds of years old. They were ennobled by long tradition; they were, too, believed to be true history. But they represented at the same time an enlarged picture of contemporary life. This seems one way of defining the Romance. It gives an idealized version of the life of the knightly class; it is the warrior's day-dream, designed for recreation (or 'solace') not instruction (or 'doctrine') and representing the average sensual man's point of view. Such stories might also reflect and celebrate contemporary events; Malory in *The Tale of the Noble King Arthur that was Emperor himself through Dignity of his Hands* seems to shadow the glorious campaigns in France in which his first lord, Richard Beauchamp, had played a heroic part. But it is quite exceptional for Romances to carry religious overtones, as in the great fourteenth-century poem of *Sir Gawayne and the Grene Knight*. In Malory, the *Tale of the Sankgreal* is a separate story, in which the religious is simply a particular department of the marvellous. Miracles or legends of the saints are the religious equivalent of the knightly Romance; the marvellous was allowed a very large share in both kinds.

Romance differs from epic in its readiness to include the fantastic, magical and wishful elements largely within the action. In epic, though the world presented is enlarged and ennobled, it remains the world of everyday. It has been suggested that the epic material of one race or culture becomes Romance when it is handed over to another race or culture and needs to be re-interpreted; when it has lost its social roots. Romance therefore presupposes epic; Malory recreates an epic story from Romance.

The hero of a medieval Romance, whatever the age in which he lived, always becomes a knight. In the Romances of Troy, Hector is described as a knight, the 'root and stock of chivalry'; Alexander becomes a medieval king. So, too, Arthur the Romano-British chieftain was seen as a contemporary ruler surrounded by his chivalry, the knights of the Round Table. The heroic early French epic of Charlemagne and the Twelve Peers of France underwent a similar transformation.

The medieval epic poem, such as Beowulf or the Song of Roland, dealt with the war leader and his band or *comitatus*; ultimately the structure of feudal society was based upon such bands, united by personal oaths of fidelity which bound vassal to lord and lord to vassal. The strong personal unity of a group of fighting men, in which unshakable loyalty and courage were essential for the merest survival, developed into the feudal state in which the barons were bound to their lord the king, the lesser tenants to their own lords, and the whole structure depended upon a network of loyalties, all of a personal kind. The society depicted in the Romances is the uppermost stratum of this social order. There is very little sense of the underlying and supporting levels of society. In Malory this is particularly noticeable. The churls who appear are churlishly treated, as when Lancelot strikes an unco-operative carter 'a reremain', a blow over the back of his neck with a mailed fist, and summarily stretches him dead. Manners consist in giving each man his due; and the Lady Lionesse thinks a kitchen knave deserves nothing but insults.

The characters in Romance are selected by age as well as class. They consist almost entirely of fighting men, their wives or mistresses, with an occasional clerk or an enchanter, a fairy or a fiend, a giant or a dwarf. Time does not work on the heroes of Malory; they may beget sons who grow up to manhood, without seeming to change in themselves: it is impossible to think of an old age, still less a late middle age, for Lancelot or Guinevere. There are very few old

**

men or women, almost no infants or children. It is also a world in which family relationships, though they exist, are usually of comparatively little significance. Fathers are finally supplanted by sons (Lancelot by Galahad, Arthur by Mordred); the relation of husband to wife is a feudal and not a personal one. Brothers are related chiefly as brothers-in-arms; sisters and mothers hardly exist. The deep relationships in this world are those of knight and vassal, or its mirror image of lady and lover; and of these, the former is in Malory the most important, the last exhibiting the same virtue of fidelity which is more amply mirrored in the comradeship of arms. There is no doubt that even in the loves of Arthur, Lancelot and Guinevere, the masculine loyalties triumph. When the strife between Gawain and Lancelot breaks out, Arthur cries:

> Wit you well, my heart was never so heavy as it is now. And much more I am sorrier for my good knights' loss than for the loss of my fair queen; for queens I might have enow, but such a fellowship of good knights shall never be together in no company.
> Vinaver, p. 833.[1]

It is mature recognition of responsibility for their guilt towards society that keeps Lancelot and Guinevere apart in the end. After Arthur is dead, and she has betaken herself to the nunnery at Amesbury, the Queen is sought out by Lancelot, and to her ladies she addresses herself before she speaks to him, and sends him away for ever:

> Through this same man and me hath all this war be wrought, and the death of the most noblest knights of the world; for through our love that we have loved together is my most noble lord slain.
> Vinaver, p. 876.

So later still Sir Lancelot laments over the two he had loved. Guinevere dies and is buried beside Arthur.

---

[1] For convenience, the page references are given to Vinaver's one-volume edition in the Oxford Standard Authors; but the spelling has been modernized throughout the quotations.

For when I remember of her beauty and her noblesse, that was both with her king and with her, so when I saw his corpse and her corpse so lie together, truly mine heart would not serve to sustain my careful body. Also when I remember me how by my defaute and mine orgule and my pride that they were both laid full low, that were peerless that ever was living of Cristen people, wit you well, said Sir Lancelot, this remembered, of their kindness and my unkindness, sank so to mine heart that I might not sustain myself.

Vinaver, p. 880.

Even such lovers as Chaucer's Troilus and Criseyde, the delicacy and complexity of whose relationship is a matter of finest adjustment, are governed instinctively by the social demands that put marriage between a prince and the widowed daughter of the traitor Calchas quite out of count. Chaucer did not need to explain this; in Malory's day, when Edward IV married Elizabeth Woodville, Warwick the Kingmaker deserted him. For Malory, the story of Lancelot and Guinevere is one of divided loyalties; it is the social results of the love even more than the love itself which concern him, while the passionate story of Tristram and Isold fails to awaken his deeper interest, and remains episodic. Here the tragic end is missing, and the lovers are left happily together at Joyous Garde, Lancelot's castle, whither they have fled.[1] This may be quite deliberate; the end of a well-known story could be suppressed to make a particular interpretation clearer, as Chaucer himself suppressed the death of Criseyde. Tristram and Isold are not faced by the same dilemma as Lancelot and Guinevere, since Mark cannot claim loyalty, being himself so treacherous; and the magic potion which they have drunk takes from their love the guilt and the glory of a voluntary choice. Theirs is a blind trancelike passion; Lancelot and Guinevere, though the Queen's stormy rages and jealous outbursts may complicate the story and drive Lancelot like Tristram over the border of madness, prove for each other a kind of fidelity

---

[1] Their end is briefly mentioned by Lancelot, as the time of his own fall draws near. (Vinaver, p. 828.)

which belongs not to the world of fancy but to the world of men.

In the great hymn in praise of fidelity in love which opens section IV of *Lancelot and Guinevere*, 'The Knight of the Cart', Malory indulges in a rare lyric outburst. True love is likened unto summer; and in words which owe nothing to his 'French book', though something perhaps to the joyous French songs which celebrate the coming of spring, he unites the love of man and woman with the great rhythms of the world and the seasons.

> . . . For, like as winter rasure doth alway arace and deface green summer, so fareth it by unstable love in man and woman, for in many persons there is no stabylité; for we may see all day, for a little blast of winter's rasure, anon we shall deface and lay apart true love, for little or naught, that cost much thing. . . .
>
> Wherefore I liken love nowadays unto summer and winter; for, like as the one is cold and the other is hot, so fareth love nowadays. And therefore all ye that be lovers, call unto your remembrance the month of May, like as did Queen Guinevere, for whom I make here a little mention, that while she lived she was a true lover, and therefore she had a good end.
>
> Vinaver, pp. 790-1.

The pathos of Malory's 'dying fall', the cadence dropping to a minor chord, is his tribute to those inward feelings which in his masculine world receive so little direct expression. As always, the supreme virtue is Truth.

The most famous and most magnificent passage in all Malory's work is the lament which closes it, the lament of Sir Ector de Maris over his brother, Sir Lancelot. Here the word 'truest, truest' sounds twice, like a tolling bell. It is the final picture of the perfect knight, the summary of all the paradoxical virtues of gentleness and sternness, all the defeated hopes that the knight prisoner had strengthened himself with in his prison.

> Ah, Lancelot! he said, thou were head of all Cristen knights! And now I dare say, said Sir Ector, thou Sir Lancelot, there thou lyest, that thou were never matched of earthly knight's hand.

And thou were the courteousest knight that ever bare shield!
And thou were the truest friend to thy lover that ever bestrad
horse, and thou were the truest lover of a sinful man that ever
loved woman, and thou were the kindest man that ever strake
with sword. And thou were the goodliest person that ever came
among press of knights, and thou was the meekest man and the
gentlest that ever ate in hall among ladies, and thou were the
sternest knight to thy mortal foe that ever put spear in the rest.

Vinaver, p. 882.

III

THE ENGLISH ROUND TABLE

If, then, the inner core of feeling which lies at the centre of Malory's world is the masculine bond of fidelity, the old loyalty of the band of fighting men, we should expect him to encounter some difficulty in dealing with the French Romances upon which his work is for the most part based, since in these the love of knight and lady was often the leading motif. The elaborate and fanciful code of manners which in theory governed the behaviour of courtly lovers, involving the absolute subjection of the knight to the lady, with all the artifice of courtly etiquette, and all the exotic ritual of a mock-religion, was never really acclimatized in England. The lovely dream of the garden of the Rose, which Guillaume de Lorris wrote and Chaucer translated, had indeed inspired some of Chaucer's love poetry; and early in the fifteenth century also had inspired that of a nobler prisoner than Malory, King James I of Scotland, who, looking out of his prison tower, beheld a fair lady walking in a spring-time garden, when

> suddenly my heart become her thrall
> For ever, of free will. . . .

But the courtly manners of royalty required a setting which most readers and writers of Romance did not know; they remade the stories, so that the kings, queens and knights became enlarged versions of themselves, with manners to correspond. Probably the most courtly poem in English about Arthur's knights is the fourteenth-century *Sir Gawayne and the Grene Knight*, in which a society as elegant as Chaucer's is depicted, and in which the manœuvring of the lady who tempts Gawain is as sophisticated as that of any heroine of Restoration comedy. A keen battle of wits between her and the knight (whom she takes at the greatest disadvantage by visiting him in bed) ends with the victory of the stronger sex; without discourtesy, Gawain repulses her, thus keeping his obligation as guest towards his host, the lady's husband.

This story was retold in rougher form as *Sir Gawayn and the Carl of Carlisle*, and here the knight's adventures with his hostess take on a much cruder and more primitive form. In some cases, courtly romances ended as popular ballads, with all the fine-drawn sentiments, all the rich descriptions pared away, to leave the simple structure, the bare bones of some tragic story, told perhaps with noble simplicity, or perhaps only with confused, dull repetition and a plentiful use of well-worn phrases. Chaucer's *Sir Thopas*, though cruel, is not unjust to the popular Romance which at its worst is unbearingly boring.

Most of these English Arthurian Romances deal with the adventures of some single knight. Sir Gawain, Sir Perceval, Sir Launcefal and the rest are each shown as the centre of a series of adventures. Some of the material belongs to the perennial world of the fairy tale; thus, tales of the fairy bride who rewards the knight with riches, with magic means to overcome his enemies, and sometimes with a fairy kingdom, are obviously popular subjects for a masculine day-dream. Other tales tell of ordeals, the overcoming of magic obstacles, or war with giants, Saracens, devils. These are the two basic forms for the Romantic adventures of a knightly hero.

In Malory, however, we meet a whole world of knights. Sir Lancelot is its undisputed champion, but Perceval, Tristram, Galahad, Gawain, Gareth and many others take for a while the centre of the stage. Malory's great work, as it would appear from the Winchester MS. which came to light in 1934 in the library of Winchester College, is a collection or anthology of tales about the Round Table. It is not a single narrative, but a group of narratives, like the *Decamerone* or the *Canterbury Tales*; based, however, on a different principle of selection—that of a common subject—all the tales are about Arthur's knights. To see the work in this way enables the reader to measure Malory's progress and his growing power in shaping his material. Caxton, when he printed the work as if it were a single continuous narrative instead of an anthology, destroyed the perspective and blurred the outlines of Malory's work. By the recovery of their plan, the stories have acquired new shape and cohesion. First to be written was *The Tale of the Noble King Arthur that was Emperor himself through Dignity of his Hands*. This is a story of military triumph in which Arthur sets out to conquer Rome; which he does, and is crowned Emperor there, thus anticipating the glories of Charlemagne among epic heroes, and reflecting for Malory the triumphant conquests of Henry V. Professor Vinaver has shown how Malory modifies the course of Arthur's French campaign to correspond with the course of Henry's. This part of Malory's work is based on an English heroic poem, *Le Morte Arthur*; but here, as in the story of Tristram, Malory has cut out the tragic ending, and uses only the first part of the poem, which deals with Arthur's triumph. At the very end of his work he was to return to another English poem to help him in depicting *The Most Piteous Tale of the Morte Arthur Saunz Guerdon*. But in the interval he relied on various 'French books', prose romances of great length, which he shaped and reorganized with increasing skill. Only for one or two stories, particularly *The Tale of Sir Gareth of Orkeney that was called Bewmaynes*, are the sources of his work unknown. To trace the history of the stories of King Arthur is a life-time's task and the majority of scholars who give themselves to the study of Malory or of his originals are concerned mainly with constructing genealogical trees for the stories and disputing various theories of descent. This, though a fascinating game, is sometimes a way of evading the duty— at once more simple and more difficult—of seeing them as literature. But the idea of the Round Table is so central to Malory's work, and in itself so especially English a development of the story, that a brief sketch of it may be attempted.

IV

MALORY AND THE HEROIC TRADITION

Three hundred years before Malory, the poet Layamon gave an account of the founding of the Table Round. Arthur held a great feast at which his vassals from Britain, Scotland, Ireland and Iceland assembled. A squabble about precedence developed in which at first bread and cups were thrown and fists used. Then a young hostage of Arthur's household snatched up the carving knives from before the King, and the killing began. It took Arthur and a hundred armed men to quell the fight, under the most terrifying threats of instant death for the men and mutilation for the women of kin to those who began the brawl. If any sought revenge for what had happened, he was to be torn in pieces by wild horses. The body of the man who began the fight was to be thrown out to rot unburied.

As a result of these measures, the dead were carried off and the feast went merrily on; but the cunning smith who offered to make Arthur a wondrous table at which sixteen hundred might sit without question of precedence seems to be catering less for the vassals of an overlord than for the members of some primitive horde. Arthur, however, appears as the dominant figure. In his words:

> Sit down! sit down at once! or your lives will pay

is heard the authentic voice of command.

Precedence at feasts, and the order of service at the lord's table was a matter of significance throughout the Middle Ages. The long narrow table on the dais in the opening scene of *Sir Gawayne and the Grene Knight* is set in customary fashion with the King in the middle, and his principal guests on each side. A round table would in fact have been a great curiosity and departure from custom, in one of those ceremonious occasions which the Romances loved to depict; and in all stories, the feast which so frequently opens or closes them (the symbol of good fellowship and unity) is described in the usual sort of medieval hall with the usual High Table on a dais. What generally happens is that the King is feasting his knights and declares that he will not eat till he sees a marvel. Instantly some damsel in distress or some strange apparition like the Green Knight appears and the adventure begins.

Although in most of the earlier Romances the story is concerned with the adventures of a particular knight, there is a sense of the brotherhood of the Round Table given by these feasts at the beginning and end of the story; after a series of combats, it is usual for the valiant enemy of the hero to be accepted as a member of the Round Table. By the fourteenth century it was thought of as a fellowship akin to that of some knightly order, such as the Garter, or the Bath, and certain kinds of tournament became known as 'round tables'.

The Great Tournament is in Malory the last and supreme moment of unity and good fellowship for the Round Table; it is the expression of the bond which is about to be disrupted by the quarrel between Lancelot and Gawain, Arthur's champion and his nephew and heir. Tournaments, or mock battles, in which knightly qualities were displayed without the risks of real battle, had become something like the Olympic Games of the fifteenth century; they were great pageants at which fortunes were spent upon equipment, and to which champions would travel from all over Europe. The last and most gorgeous occasion of this kind to be generally remembered is the encounter between Henry VIII and the King of France, known as the Field of the Cloth of Gold.

Such tournaments gave opportunity for the writer of Romance to indulge in long descriptions of splendour, with detailed accounts of the dishes at the feasts, the armour of the knights and the order of combat. Here Malory departs from the habits of the age. He is not interested in descriptions but in action; and he does not do more than note the colour of the knights' armour. The foining and tracing of combat excites him, but his world lacks the stateliness and the ritual of Chaucer's and the Gawain poet's, the true courtly ceremoniousness.

He has, on the other hand, a very strong sense of the Fellowship which enables him to rise to the heights of the last books. This sense of the Fellowship dominates one or two other works; such as the poem of *Lancelot du Laik* and the alliterative *Morte Arthur* on which Malory based the first of his tales. These poems imitate the literary form of the Chronicle History. Here there is an account of the King's challenge to lordship of a foreign land; then an invasion and a series of battles are described, very closely akin to the English wars in France. In each battle, a list of the eminent warriors taking part on both sides is given, and a list of those who fell. Such poems are no longer pure Romance of adventure; they are histories. In Malory, too, there is this strong sense of history, implying the epic rather than the Romance style.

After his early tale of Arthur's conquest of Rome, Malory turned back for a time to the more primitive and wilder stories about Merlin. These belong to the oldest traditions of Romance. In general, the more primitive the stories, the larger the part played by magic; thus in the one Arthurian tale which occurs in the *Mabinogion*, all the knights are possessed of superhuman powers, and are frankly figures of magical rather than human kind.

After his excursion into the realms of magic, Malory tells a number of tales about individual knights, in the same form roughly as the Romances of adventure which have been described. These are tales of wanderings, in which the hero rides away on a quest. The quest for the Sankgreal includes five such tales of individual knights. The tragic tale of *The knight with the Two Swords* and the tale of Gareth have each a strong and shapely coherence; others follow rather the interlacing and interweaving technique of the long French romances. The story of Tristram is of this kind, containing in itself several minor stories, such as the tale of Alexander le Orphelin.

The adventures of individual knights in their quests show them freed from all restrictions of ordinary life. Armour and tournaments may be realistic, but in a Romance there is suppression of all the usual laws of cause and effect in action. The knightly champion has to meet giants, dragons, monsters, the King's enemies, sorcerers and mysteries of all kinds. Heads that are cut off may be stuck on again; marvels and wonders are the rule and not the exception. The appearance and manners of the knight are familiar, merely an enlargement of the everyday, but he has no responsibilities, no followers, he rides through vast and shadowy landscapes and forests, where only the cities of Caerleon and Carlisle remind the listener that this is England. The modern reader may see a parallel in the world of science fiction, in which the admired technical apparatus which commands most prestige today is used to decorate the wildest fantasy. Romance indulges in the same mixture of the fanciful and the up-to-date. It allows the listener to identify himself with a hero of almost superhuman prowess, yet matches him against forces which stress his humanity and normality. Monsters from Mars are the modern equivalent of the fairy-tale giant.

Most romances of individual knights arrive at a happy ending; feasts and weddings wind them up. When the theme is the Table Round itself, however, the story ends with the great epic battle, the unsuccessful fight against odds. Whereas incidents of the individual Romances defy cause and effect, in the epic of the Round Table morality is always felt behind the action; the ideal is a social and ethical one. It was to this graver subject that Malory finally attained at the end of his work, joining the tale of his great hero Lancelot with the fate of the whole Fellowship.

The stories of Arthur and his knights can thus be seen to undergo a development not unrelated to the society which in an idealized form they reflect. In the earliest tales, magic and violence predominate; then the image of a society based on feudal ties of loyalty emerges; the adventures of individuals follow, with, in the more courtly versions, much stress on manners and on wooing, and in the popular versions, simply on adventure and marvels. In both, the ideal knight in quest of adventure undergoes a great variety of different trials, from which he usually emerges victorious. Finally, something akin to the older epic style reappears, reflecting also the form of contemporary chronicles and, in Malory, tinged with some shadowing from contemporary struggles. At his greatest, in the final passages dealing with the last battle and death of Arthur, he seems to reflect in an enlarged form all the troubles of his own society, the ruin which civil strife had brought upon him and his kind. This is imaginatively seen in the dissolution of the Table Round, the bond and fellowship of knighthood. Conquest, like true and faithful love, belongs to the past: the first and last campaigns of Arthur represent for Malory a youthful hope of the past contrasted with a tragic present.

V

TRAGIC THEMES IN MALORY

Malory was, of course, not depicting the troubles of his time directly; he was giving an imaginative form to them only. Unlike the poets of the alliterative tradition, Langland and the rest, he has no counsel to give. The grace and beauty of the *Morte Darthur* spring largely from its freedom from any reflection, any complicated tangle of social or of emotional repercussions. It is a splendid holiday from all such teasing questions as our living in the daily world implies.

The fights are sheer trials of strength and skill; the love-making is as free from sentimentality, complaint, or evasion as the healthy union of animals. There is something extra-ordinarily clean about Malory's world. Nearly all the knights are good except Kay (who appears chiefly in the early books), Mark, Mordred and a few characters like Breuntz sauns Pitié; but these are so clearly labelled, and their churlishness is so obvious, that the listener is quite untroubled by their fulfilling of their customary roles. Morgan le Fay, the wicked Queen and Arthur's sister, is the villainess of the piece, a figure at once more remote and more powerful.

Blood flows very freely. Two strange knights meet, 'and as soon as either saw other they made them ready to joust'. When they had fought for half a day and nearly killed each other, they ask each other's name and discover that they are Sir Perceval and Sir Ector de Maris, both in search of Sir Lancelot, who has run mad in the woods. Both feel themselves to be dying and are unable even to seek a priest for shriving. But Perceval kneels and prays, and on a sudden appearance of the Sankgreal 'forthwith they were as whole of hide and limb as ever they were in their life' (Vinaver, p. 603). An action which resembles nothing so much as the instinctive rushing together of two

wild boars (Malory's favourite simile for his warriors) thus
ends with a miracle that does not at all differ from the magic
spells of the Lady Lionesse, who restored the heads of de-
capitated knights by enchantment. The knights are suitably
chastened:

> Then they gave thankings to God with great mildness

and gravely discuss what can have happened to them. Sir
Ector explains to Sir Perceval that they have seen the Holy
Grail.

> 'So God me help', said Sir Perceval, 'I saw a damsel, as me
> thought, all in white, with a vessel in both her hands, and forth-
> with I was whole.'
>
> So then they took their horses and their harness, and mended
> it as well as they might that was broken; and so they mounted
> up and rode talking together. And there Sir Ector de Maris told
> Sir Perceval how that he had sought his brother Sir Lancelot, long,
> and never could hear witting of him: 'In many hard adventures
> have I been in this quest.' And so either told other of their great
> adventures.   Vinaver, pp. 603-4.

This condition of complete simplicity, a combination of
violence and innocence, was presumably taken for granted
by Malory himself and by his contemporaries. Vinaver
points out how new is delight in the inarticulate assurance
of the fighting man when King Arthur asks his knights for
counsel. 'They had no counsel, but said they were big
enough.' There is pathos in the loyalty of Sir Lancelot's
kinsmen, when they warn him 'insomuch as ye were taken
with her, whether ye did right other wrong, it is now your
part to hold with the queen', and he asks them 'Wherefore,
my fair lords, my kin and my friends, what will ye do?'

> And anon they said all with one voice:
> 'We will do as ye will do'   Vinaver, p. 827.

Taciturnity could go no further than the comment of
the hermit when his salutary counsel to do penance is

rejected by Gawain, on the plea that the life of a knight-errant is sufficiently hard in itself.

> 'Well' said the good man and then he held his peace.
>
> Vinaver, p. 651.

'Tacit et fecit' might be the motto of any of Arthur's knights.

A knight finds his mother in bed with another knight. He strikes off her head. A lady whose knight is slain kills herself with his sword. Elaine gets Lancelot to her bed by enchantment, even within Arthur's court, and knowing that he thinks he is abed with Guinevere. Such a trick, which destroys all depth in the action when Shakespeare uses it in *All's Well that Ends Well* and *Measure for Measure*, does not jar in Malory. He comments:

> And wit you well this lady was glad, and so was Sir Lancelot for he wende that he had had another in his arms. Vinaver, p. 593.

After Lancelot has fled, being driven mad by the anger of Guinevere, the two ladies from mutual reproaches fall to common lament.

> 'As for that' said dame Elaine, 'I dare undertake he is marred for ever, and that have you made. For neither you nor I are like to rejoice him, for he made the most piteous groans when he leapt out at yonder bay window that ever I heard man make. Alas!' said fair Elaine, and 'Alas!' said the queen, 'for now I wot well that we have lost him for ever.' Vinaver, p. 595.

It is left to Sir Bors to rebuke both of them; he spares neither Elaine nor the Queen, who proceeds to send out knights in quest for Lancelot, with 'treasure enough' for their expenses—a fact that is duly recorded to Lancelot himself when he returns to his right mind.

> 'And therefore, brother' said Sir Ector 'make you ready to ride to the court with us. And I dare say, and make it good,' said Sir Ector 'it hath cost my lady the Queen twenty thousand pounds the seeking of you.' Vinaver, p. 616.

This, as Vinaver observed, is the only time an Arthurian quest is assessed in money terms. There's beggary in the love that can be reckoned, as Antony says, but perhaps it is not unfitting that one who knew the inside of a debtor's prison should use the hateful unfamiliar terms for once, to reckon the worth of Lancelot.

Set against Elaine the mother of Galahad, is Elaine the Maid of Astolat, whose story is perhaps the most inward and pathetic of all Malory's tales. Elaine of Astolat shares with her young brother Lavaine a kind of compulsive and enthralled devotion to Lancelot; it is at once completely innocent and frankly sensuous. She speaks to Lancelot in the voice of Miranda.

> 'Why, what would ye that I did?' said Sir Lancelot.
> 'Sir, I would have you to my husband' said Elaine.
> 'Fair damsel, I thank you heartily', said Sir Lancelot, 'but truly', said he 'I cast me never to be wedded man.'
> 'Then fair knight', said she, 'will ye be my paramour?'
> 'Jesu defend me!' said Sir Lancelot 'For then I rewarded your father and your brother full evil for their great goodness.'
> 'Alas then' said she 'I must die for your love.'
>
> Vinaver, p. 777.

Lancelot's attempt at consolation is a model of tactlessness. He informs her that he has had many other offers, and says that he would like to reward her for her kindness, which he will do by settling upon her a dowry of a thousand pounds a year.

And so he departs, attended by Lavaine:

> 'Father' said sir Lavaine 'I dare make good she is a clean maiden as for my lord sir Lancelot; but she doth as I do, for sithen I first saw my lord sir Lancelot I could never depart from him, neither nought I will, and I may follow him.'   Vinaver, p. 778.

The death of Elaine, justifying her love against the counsel of her ghostly father, who bade her leave such thoughts ('Why should I leave such thoughts? am I not an earthly woman?') but submitting herself to God, is perhaps a more truly religious occasion than all the episodes of the Holy Grail. There is the clearest acceptance of bodily death; she asks her brother to write a letter 'and while my body is hot let this letter be put in my right hand, and my hand bound fast to the letter until that I be cold'. This letter containing her plaint to Lancelot and her last request that he would bury her and offer her mass-penny is delivered in the scene that is the most dramatically and picturesquely described in all Malory; the barge hung in black samite, hove to upon the Thames; the silent boatman; and the corpse on a fair bed, covered to her middle with cloth of gold.

> And she lay as she had smiled.   Vinaver, p. 780.

Death is the one fact which is emotionally charged in Malory. Again and again, when he records the deaths of Balin, of Gawain, of Arthur and finally of Lancelot he rises to heights of passion and of eloquence which cannot be matched elsewhere in the *Morte Darthur*. Although life is cheap and wounds are so frequent that the chief knights seem to be sorely wounded about an average of once a week, yet in the moment of death which is also the moment of truth, a life may be summed up, a judgment given, and a garland bestowed.

In the last tales, the emotionally charged fact of death and the imaginatively perceived disruption of the social order are combined, as Malory describes the mutual destruction of the Table Round and the death of his chief heroes. There is still nothing that could be called reflection, comment or entanglement in daily living; there is, of course, the fully apprehended physical horror of battle.

> Then sir Lucan took up the king the one party and sir Bedwere the other party, and in the lifting up the king swooned and in the lifting sir Lucan fell in a swoon, that parts of his guts fell out of his body. . . . And when the king awoke, he behold sir Lucan how he lay foaming at the mouth and part of his guts lay at his feet.
> Vinaver, p. 869.

But beyond this, there is the deeper pain that arises from remorse, from the failing of the Fellowship, and above all from the sense of mystery, which comes with the passing of Arthur in the black barge tended by the weeping Queens. The good end of Lancelot and of Guinevere, and of the remnant of the knights, who took the Cross and 'died upon a Good Friday for God's sake'—the last words of the book—are in the nature of a *coda*. For the men and women of Malory are earthly men and women; and for them, the good life of earth, the active life of loving and fighting, the unharboured heaths and the unlimited horizons of Arthur's kingdom are all in all.

VI

THE DAY OF DESTINY

The ancient heroic tradition of English poetry—the tradition of *Beowulf* and of *The Battle of Maldon*—descended to Malory through the English alliterative poetry of the fourteenth century upon which he based his earliest story, *The Tale of the Noble King Arthur that was Emperor himself through Dignity of his Hands*. His own shaping of the Arthurian tales, which had already undergone so many Protean changes in the course of the three hundred years in which they had been the common property of writers all over Western Europe, was grave, masculine, and at its deepest levels concerned with personal relationships as part of the social structure and not as the private, secret joy and pain of man or woman. Elaine of Astolat, though a touching is yet a minor figure in his great tapestry. The French books had developed the subtlety and the fineness of courtly love, and had overlaid the stories' primitive simplicities. The author of *Sir Gawayne and the Grene Knight* had fused adventure and morality; at the centre of his poem is a description of the emblem of the Five Wounds of Christ and the Five Joys of Mary which the good knight bears upon his shield. Malory's world is rougher and simpler than either of these. In the last two tales, *The Book of Sir Lancelot and Queen Guinevere* and *The Most Piteous Tale of the Morte Arthur Saunz Guerdon*, he attains to his full heroic theme.

In the intervening tales, his characters had acquired a kind of depth and stability which the figures of English Romances do not usually possess. Where interest is concentrated upon a marvellous succession of adventures, characters retain a fairy-tale flatness and remain simply types, upon which the fantasy of the listeners can be easily projected, and with whom they can readily identify themselves. The central figure in the warrior's day-dream must be fairly indeterminate, if he is to act as an idealized self for all and sundry. Slowly, Arthur, Gawain and Lancelot have become, if not characters in the full dramatic sense, at least figures defined by their existence in a mutual relationship to each other. They have social if not individual identities.

In *The Tale of the Noble King Arthur*, it is the King himself who is the hero of the tale. Here, instead of a quest, Malory depicts a whole campaign. There is nevertheless a magnificent preliminary description of Arthur's single-handed combat with the giant of St. Michael's Mount. A weird and terrifying scene first greets him as he climbs to the summit of the crag—a weeping woman by a new-made grave, two fires 'flaming high' at which the bodies of little children, 'broched in a manner like birds' are being roasted and tended by three captive damsels. In such setting is a tremendous hand-to-hand encounter. At the end of this, locked together, the King and the sorely wounded giant roll from the top to the bottom of the mountain.

> With that the warlow wrath Arthur under, and so they waltred and tumbled over the crags and bushes, and either cleght other full fast in their arms. And other whiles Arthur was above and other whiles under, and so weltering and wallowing they rolled down the hill, and they never left till they fell thereas the flood marked. But ever in the waltring Arthur smites and hits him with a short dagger up to the hilts, and in his falling there brast of the giant's ribs three even at once.   Vinaver, p. 147.

The rough wit by which he is greeted by his comrades 'I have mickle wonder and Michael be of such making, that ever God would suffer him to abide in Heaven' is matched by Arthur's own, when in the fight with the Emperor he cuts off a giant by the knees: ' "Now art thou of a size" said the king "like unto our fairies" and then he struck off his head swiftly' (Vinaver, p. 159). But the King's prowess having been established in his fight with the giant, others are permitted a large share in the victorious advance upon Rome.

In Arthur's campaign there is the first glimmering of a

national pride, which was quite foreign to the knightly society of the Middle Ages, and to the medieval Romance. It is manifest in the opening scenes, with the brilliant picture of an invading fleet setting out from England and making its way across to France. Only in the first and the last of the Tales does geography become significant; and it does so because in both these parts of the story Malory is depicting the fate, not of individuals, but of a nation.

At the end there is a regression from the more civilized social bonds of the Fellowship to the primitive ones of kinship. In the final books, rival brotherhoods to that of the Table Round appear. It is the five nephews of Arthur who in different ways oppose Lancelot—Aggravayne and Mordred by treachery, Gawain, Gaherys and Gareth from mischance. These last dissociate themselves strongly from the plots of the other two, who lead a little band of twelve 'and they were of Scotland, other else of Sir Gawain's kin, other well-willers to his brother.' On the other hand, Lancelot's danger draws together 'all we that ben of your blood and your well-willers' as Sir Bors tells him. Roused by a common sense of alarm, they had all wakened from sleep and come together at the moment when the treacherous assault upon the Queen's chamber was made. The issue is clear to Lancelot.

> 'And therefore, my fellows' said Sir Lancelot, 'I pray you all that ye will be of heart good, and help me in what need that ever I stand, for now is war comen to us all.'
>
> 'Sir' said Sir Bors 'all is welcome that God sendeth us, and as we have taken much weal with you and much worship, we will take the woe with you as we have taken the weal.'
>
> And therefore they said, all the good knights.
>
> 'Look ye, take no discomfort! for there is no bond of knights under heaven but we shall be able to grieve them as much as they us, and therefore discomfort not yourself by no manner. And we shall gather together all that we love and that loveth us, and what that ye will have done shall be done. And therefore let us take the woe and the joy together.' Vinaver, p. 825.

The knightly virtue of loyalty has turned against itself. From this point all the efforts of Lancelot to avoid that war which he knows is inevitable are doomed. Gawain refuses to oppose Lancelot; as a consequence his two younger brothers, sent as guards to the Queen's trial, and going reluctantly and unarmed, are slain unawares by Lancelot in his rescue of the Queen; and so the blood feud between himself and Gawain begins. Gawain denies what he well knows, that the deaths were sheer mischance; Lancelot will not defend himself at the cost of injury to Arthur or Gawain; he makes the most stupendous offers of penance for the deaths of Gaherys and Gareth, including a pilgrimage barefoot and in his shirt, from Sandwich to Carlisle, but Gawain will not be reconciled.

Lancelot is first besieged in Joyous Garde and then, when it cannot be reduced, banished the realm; to point the moral, here in his lament ancient examples of a tragic fall are evoked.

> 'Fortune is so variant, and the wheel so mutable, that there is no constant abiding. And that may be proved by many old chronicles, as of noble Ector of Troy and Alysaunder, the mighty conqueror, and many mo other. . . .'   Vinaver, p. 847.

So Sir Lancelot departs to Bayonne, and Arthur and his knights once more invade France, no longer as conquerors but in pursuit of Gawain's crazed revenge. Then swiftly follows the treachery of Mordred, Arthur's nephew and bastard son, gotten upon his sister Morgawse, Queen of Orkney. Mordred, left as regent in England, revolts against Arthur. The sin at the heart of Arthur's court is finally embodied in this dark figure. The fruitless attempt to destroy Lancelot fails, and Gawain dies repentant; the final battle, that between Arthur and the dark powers, draws on. Even here, at the last moment, a bid is made for peace; Arthur and Mordred hold a parley between the hosts, but each in such mistrust that they warn their followers if any sword is drawn, they should advance and slay. Success is actually achieved; but Fortune turns her wheel, and the Day of Destiny falls upon the chivalry of Britain.

> And so they met as their poyntement was, and were agreed and accorded thoroughly. And wine was fetched and they drank together. Right so came out an adder of a little heath bush, and it stung a knight in the foot. And so when the knight felt him so stung, he looked down and saw the adder; and anon he drew his sword to slay the adder, and thought none other harm. And when the host on both parties saw that sword drawn, then they blew beams, trumpets and horns, and shouted grimly, and so both hosts dressed them togethers. And King Arthur took his horse and said 'Alas, this unhappy day!' and so rode to his party, and Sir Mordred in like wise.
>
> Vinaver, p. 867.

There is very little left of either host by the end of the day, when the father and son confront each other, afoot and weary, over the heaps of dead, and Arthur drives his spear through Mordred's body, while Mordred thrusts himself forward to the butt end of the spear, to give Arthur his death's wound by the sword.

The growth of treachery and mistrust, and the vanity of all efforts by men to stay the course of Fortune's wheel as it whirls them down to destruction give to these last books of the *Morte Darthur* an ironic unity and a singleness of action which are new to Malory, and far beyond the world of Romance. He had achieved something of the same effect upon a smaller scale in his early tale of *Balin or the Knight with Two Swords*. Balin, a knight out of wild Northumberland, rough and uncouth, by his impulsive acts of vengeance brings down ruin upon himself and his house. Confronted by magic dangers, and invisible foes, he is a human figure imposed on a legendary background, whose very confusion and portentous horror enhances his rude and simple courage. Throughout the story the sense of doom is felt in the phrase so often applied to Balin, 'he may not long endure'; in his last battle he rides forward at the challenging sound of the horn, with so ominous and savage a comparison that he seems like Roland riding to the Dark Tower.

> And so he heard an horn blow as it had been the death of a beast. 'That blast' said Balyn, 'is blowen for me, for I am the prize and yet am I not dead.'
> Vinaver, p. 67.

So he goes forward into combat, only to find, in the hour of death, that he has fought his own brother Balan, and that they have slain each other.

The slaying of the kinsman, here as in Arthur's last battle, is an act at once profoundly unnatural and yet felt to be inevitable; it marks the disruption of the last and deepest social bond. What symbolism might be seen in this act by more sophisticated ages is irrelevant to Malory, whose greatness lies in his literal significance, and in the boldness with which he faces the unshirkable mysteries of anger and fidelity, courage and grief, love and death. In Arthur's death-scene there is a foreshadowing of Shakespeare's tableau in *Henry VI*: the civil strife, the lamenting King who is also the father killing the son, while the son also kills the father. Whether in the single story of Balin, or in the ruin of a kingdom, it is in depicting heroic tragic action that Malory attains his full stature. There are more purely Romantic pleasures to be gained from his work, including, even for modern readers, the pleasures of the day-dream; but there is no sickliness in his dreams, as there is no malice in his violence. His is a mirror of the Active Life, untouched by Contemplation.

SIR THOMAS MALORY

Select Bibliography

BIBLIOGRAPHIES

"A Bibliography of Critical Arthurian Literature" is published annually in *Modern Language Quarterly* (1940—in progress).

There is a bibliography in *The Works of Sir Thomas Malory*. Edited by Eugène Vinaver, 1947 (see below).

For further bibliographical aids, see the preface to *Arthurian Literature in the Middle Ages: A Collaborative History*. Edited by Roger S. Loomis, 1959 (see below).

EDITIONS

The Noble and Ioyous Book Entytled Le Morte Darthur Notwythstondying It Treateth of the Byrth Lyf and Actes of the Sayd Kyng Arthur of his Noble Knyghtes of the Rounde Table Theyr Mervayllous Enquestes and Adventures Thachyevyng of the Sankgreal and in Thende the Dolorous Deth and Departyng Out of Thys World of Them Al Whiche Booke was Reduced in to Engylsshe by Syr Thomas Malory Knyght. Westminster: William Caxton, 1485.

Of this first edition only two copies are recorded (Rylands and Pierpont Morgan Libraries). Only two copies (Rylands and Oxford) are recorded of the second edition, printed by Wynkyn de Worde at Westminster in 1498.

Le Morte Darthur. Edited by H. Oska Sommer. 3 vols. London: David Nutt, 1889–1891.

A line by line reprint of the first edition of 1485, with a long introduction, glossary, and study of sources.

The Works of Sir Thomas Malory. Edited by Eugène Vinaver. 3 vols. Oxford: Clarendon Press, 1947.

The standard edition, the first to be based on the unique Winchester manuscript. Contains a bibliography, introduction, commentary, glossary. For some criticism of this edition, see especially Robert H. Wilson,

"How Many Books did Malory Write?" *University of Texas Studies in English*, XXX (1951).

The Works of Sir Thomas Malory. Edited by Eugène Vinaver. Oxford Standard Authors. London and New York: Oxford University Press, 1954.
Practically the same text as the preceding, in one volume, without the critical apparatus, but with a brief introduction and glossary. The handiest edition.

The Tale of the Death of King Arthur. Edited by Eugène Vinaver. Oxford: Clarendon Press, 1955.
A revised portion of Vinaver's standard 3 vol. edition, forming a good introduction to the study of Malory.

MODERNIZATIONS

Le Morte Darthur. Preface by Sir John Rhys. Everyman's Library. New York: E. P. Dutton, 1906.
Frequently reprinted. Caxton's text modernized, with a glossary.

Le Morte Darthur. Modernized by A. W. Pollard. 2 vols. New York: University Books, 1962.
First published in 1902.

BIOGRAPHICAL AND CRITICAL STUDIES OF MALORY AND STUDIES OF ARTHURIAN ROMANCE

MAYNARDIER, GUSTAVUS H. *Arthur of the English Poets.* Boston: Houghton Mifflin, 1907.
A study of the influence of Malory upon subsequent writers.

SCUDDER, VIDA D. *Le Morte Darthur of Sir Thomas Malory and Its Sources.* New York: E. P. Dutton, 1917.
A general study.

BRUCE, JAMES D. *The Evolution of Arthurian Romance from Its Beginnings Down to the Year 1300.* Hesperia. 2 vols. Baltimore: The Johns Hopkins Press, 1923.
A monumental study, not now the most authoritative (see Loomis, Roger S., ed. below).

CHAMBERS, EDMUND K. *Arthur of Britain.* London: Sidgwick and Jackson, 1927.
A more condensed study of Arthurian legend.

HICKS, EDWARD. *Sir Thomas Malory: His Turbulent Career. A Biography.* Cambridge: Harvard University Press, 1928.

VINAVER, EUGÈNE. *Sir Thomas Malory*. Oxford: Clarendon Press, 1929.
A general study, written before the discovery of the Winchester manuscript in 1934.

MACNEICE, LOUIS. "Sir Thomas Malory," *The English Novelists*. Edited by Derek Verschoyle. New York: Harcourt, Brace, 1936.

BREWER, D. S. "Form in the *Morte Darthur*," *Medium Ævum*, XXI (1952).

LOOMIS, ROGER S. "Edward I, Arthurian Enthusiast," *Speculum*, XXVIII (1953).

LOOMIS, ROGER S., ed. *Arthurian Literature in the Middle Ages: A Collaborative History*. Oxford: Clarendon Press, 1959.
A new and authoritative survey of the vast field of Arthurian literature by thirty scholars.

FERGUSON, ARTHUR B. *The Indian Summer of English Chivalry: Studies in the Decline and Transformation of Chivalric Idealism*. Durham: Duke University Press, 1960.

BENNETT, J. A. W., ed. *Essays on Malory*. Oxford: Clarendon Press, 1963.

RECORDING

The Cambridge Treasury of English Prose: Volume I, Malory to Donne. Caedmon–TC 1054.

MEDIEVAL LITERATURE IN GENERAL AND RELATED BACKGROUND STUDIES

Select Bibliography

TRANSLATIONS AND EDITIONS OF SOME MEDIEVAL WORKS

English

The Babees Book: Manners and Meals in Olden Time. Edited by F. J. Furnivall. Early English Text Society, 1868.
There is a modernization by Edith Rickert (New York: Duffield, 1908)

GOWER, JOHN. *The Complete Works.* Edited by G. C. Macaulay. 4 vols. Oxford: Clarendon Press, 1899–1902.
Gower's English poem, *Confessio Amantis,* is translated by Terence Tiller (Baltimore: Penguin Books, 1963).

JULIANA OF NORWICH. *Revelations of Divine Love.* Edited by Dom Roger Huddleston, O. S. B. Orchard Books. Westminster, Md.: Newman Press, 1952.
There is a translation by James Walsh (London: Burns and Oates, 1961).

LANGLAND, WILLIAM. *Piers the Plowman.* Edited by Walter W. Skeat. 2 vols. Oxford: Clarendon Press, 1886.
The fullest edition. Convenient to use is *Piers the Plowman: A Critical Edition of the A-Version.* Edited by T. A. Knott and David C. Fowler (Baltimore: The Johns Hopkins Press, 1952). A complete new critical edition is under way, the first volume of which is edited by George Kane (London: Athlone Press, 1960). There is a complete prose translation by J. F. Goodridge (Baltimore: Penguin Books, 1959), and a partial verse translation by Nevill Coghill (New York: Oxford University Press, 1950).

Religious Lyrics of the XIVth Century. Edited by Carleton Brown. Oxford: Clarendon Press, 1924.

Religious Lyrics of the XVth Century. Edited by Carleton Brown. Oxford: Clarendon Press, 1939.

Secular Lyrics of the XIVth and XVth Centuries. Edited by Rossell H. Robbins. Oxford: Clarendon Press, 1952.

Sir Gawain and the Green Knight. Edited by J. R. R. Tolkien and E. V. Gordon. Oxford: Clarendon Press, 1925.
There is a verse translation by Brian Stone (Baltimore: Penguin Books, 1959).

York Plays. Edited by Lucy Toulmin Smith. Oxford: Clarendon Press, 1885.
A new edition is expected soon, by Arthur Brown for the Early English Text Society. There is a nearly complete verse translation by Canon J. S. Purvis (London: S. P. C. K., 1957).

Fourteenth Century Verse and Prose. Edited by Kenneth Sisam. Oxford: Clarendon Press, 1921.
Frequently reprinted. Standard introduction, full glossary.

The Age of Chaucer. Edited by William Frost. English Masterpieces Vol. I. Englewood Cliffs, N. J.: Prentice Hall, 1950. 2nd ed. 1961.
An introductory volume, simpler than *Fourteenth Century Verse and Prose* (the previous item above).

European

ANDREAS CAPELLANUS. *The Art of Courtly Love.* Translated by John J. Parry. New York: Columbia University Press, 1941.

Les Art Poètiques du XII⁰ et du XIII⁰ Siècle. Edited by Edmond Faral. Paris: Champion, 1924.
An edition and account of medieval treatises on rhetoric.

BOETHIUS. *The Consolation of Philosophy.* Translated with introduction and notes by Richard Green. The Library of Liberal Arts. Indianapolis: Bobbs-Merrill, 1962.
Chaucer's own translation of *The Consolation of Philosophy* is in Robinson's edition of Chaucer.

DANTE ALIGHIERI. *The Convivia.* Translated by P. H. Wicksteed. The Temple Classics. London: Dent, 1924.

———. *The Divine Comedy.* Translated by John D. Sinclair. 3 vols. New York: Oxford University Press, 1948.
Prose translation facing the Italian. Commentary.

———. *The Portable Dante*. Edited by Paolo Milano. New York: Viking Press, 1947.
Paperback. Includes *The Divine Comedy* complete. Commentary.

LORRIS, GUILLAUME DE, AND JEAN DE MEUN. *The Romance of the Rose*. Translated by Harry W. Robbins. New York: Dutton, 1962.
The partial Middle English translation, some of which is by Chaucer, is in Robinson's edition of Chaucer.

JONES, CHARLES W., ed. *Medieval Literature in Translation*. New York: Longmans, Green, 1950.
Standard large anthology.

GENERAL BACKGROUND STUDIES

ANDERSON, M. D. *The Medieval Carver*. New York: Macmillan, 1935.

BETHURUM, DOROTHY, ed. *Critical Approaches to Medieval Literature*. Selected papers from the English Institute, 1958–1959. New York: Columbia University Press, 1960.

COOK, G. H. *Mediaeval Chantries and Chantry Chapels*. Letchworth, Herts: Phoenix House, 1947.

DAVIS, HENRY W. C., ed. *Mediaeval England*. Oxford: Clarendon Press, 1924.
A useful companion to literary studies; with chapters on architecture, trade, costume, etc.

EVANS, JOAN. *English Art 1307–1461*. Oxford: Clarendon Press, 1949.

HARVEY, JOHN H. *Henry Yevele: The Life of an English Architect*. New York: Batsford, 1944.

HUIZINGA, JOHAN. *The Waning of the Middle Ages*. London: Arnold, 1924; Penguin Books, 1955.

JACKSON, WILLIAM THOMAS H. *The Literature of the Middle Ages*. New York: Columbia University Press, 1960.

JACOB, ERNEST F. *The Fifteenth Century*. The Oxford History of England. Oxford: Clarendon Press, 1961.

JUSSERAND, J. J. *English Wayfaring Life in the Middle Ages*. Translated by Lucy Toulmin Smith. New ed. rev. and enlarged by the author. London: T. F. Unwin, 1920; 4th ed. New York: Putnam, 1950.

LEWIS, C. S. *The Allegory of Love*. Oxford: Clarendon Press, 1938.
Extended account of "Courtly Love."

McKISACK, MAY. *The Fourteenth Century*. The Oxford History of England. Oxford: Clarendon Press, 1959.

OWST, GERALD R. *Literature and Pulpit in Mediaeval England.* Cambridge: University Press, 1933; 2nd ed. New York: Barnes and Noble, 1961.

POWER, EILEEN. *Mediaeval People.* 9th ed. New York: Barnes and Noble, 1950.

RICKERT, MARGARET. *Painting in Britain: The Middle Ages.* The Pelican History of Art. Baltimore: Penguin Books, 1954.

ROBERTSON, D. W., JR. *A Preface to Chaucer: Studies in Medieval Perspectives.* Princeton: Princeton University Press, 1962.
An important, substantial, and controversial introduction to Chaucer's intellectual and artistic background.

STONE, LAWRENCE. *Sculpture in Britain: The Middle Ages.* The Pelican History of Art. Baltimore: Penguin Books, 1955.

TAYLOR, HENRY OSBORN. *The Mediaeval Mind.* 2 vols. London: Macmillan, 1911; 4th ed. Cambridge: Harvard University Press, 1951.

TREVELYAN, G. M. *Illustrated English Social History.* 4 vols. New York: Longman, Green, 1949–1952.
Vol. I contains a colored reproduction of the Corpus Christi College MS referred to at the end of Professor Coghill's essay on Chaucer.

─────────

Further studies and reference works are listed in: *The Cambridge Bibliography of English Literature,* 4 vols. (1941) and *Supplement* (1957); the Annual Bibliographies published in *PMLA* by the Modern Language Association of America; *The Year's Work in English Studies,* a survey of important critical books and articles, published annually for the English Association by Oxford University Press; the *Annual Bibliography of English Language and Literature,* an extensive listing of critical books and articles, published for the Modern Humanities Research Association by Cambridge University Press; the Bibliographies of Periodical Literature published in each issue of the quarterly *Speculum: A Journal of Mediaeval Studies;* and *A Manual of the Writings in Middle English* by John E. Wells (New Haven: Yale University Press, 1916), which with its nine supplements (the last published in 1952) is complete to 1945.